THE MAGIC OF TREES

Exhibition:
November 21, 1998–April 5, 1999

THE MAGIC OF TREES

With a Foreword by Ernst Beyeler

Texts by
Markus Brüderlin, Bernhard Gardi,
Reinhold Hohl, Christian Kaufmann

FONDATION **BEYELER**

Acknowledgements

Lenders

Special thanks is due to all those who stood by us with help and advice during the preparations for this exhibition: Esti Dunow, Dorothee Fischer, Rainer Hüben, Annely Juda, Dr. Dieter Koepplin, Paul Müller, Dr. Christian Rümelin, Rüdiger Schöttle, Prof. Paul Tucker and Wolfgang Wittrock.

We would like to express our sincere appreciation to the artists who contributed installations to the exhibition, among them Hamish Fulton, Wolfgang Laib and Giuseppe Penone. We are also very grateful to Bernd Steiner from The International Tree Archives in Winterthur for the photographic documentation "Bäume" and to Martin Fäh for the media installation in the Greenpeace/WWF information tent.
We are much indebted to Hugo Lipp, Thomas Schaffner, Ernst Schläpfer and Dominik Zurfluh for their help in setting up the exhibition. We are also grateful to Luciano Frohoff and Daniel Grütter of the Möbel-Transport AG, Basle, for their effort and logistic care taking. Finally, we would like to extend our gratitude to the company Bodenbau AG, Allschwil, for sponsoring material required for the Wolfgang Laib installation.

We would like to extend our gratitude to the numerous private lenders and all of the participating museums for their valuable loans:

Art & Public, Geneva
Foundation E. G. Bührle Collection, Zurich
Carnegie Museum of Art, Pittsburgh
Christo and Jeanne-Claude
Succession Gérald Cramer, Geneva
Collection L. Declerck, Belgium
Donald Young Gallery, Chicago
Fondation Dubuffet, Paris
Fondation Marguerite et Aimé Maeght, Saint-Paul
Collection Hamish Fulton
Collection Gemeentemuseum, The Hague, The Netherlands
Galerie Konrad Fischer, Düsseldorf
Galerie Karsten Greve, Cologne, Paris, Milan
Reuben and Edith Hecht Museum, University of Haifa, Israel
Kirchner Museum, Davos
Kröller-Müller Museum, Otterlo
Kunsthaus Zürich
Kunstmuseum Bern
Kunstmuseum Bonn, permanent loan from Sammlung Hans Grothe
Kunstmuseum Luzern
Kunstmuseum Solothurn
Kunstsammlung Nordrhein-Westfalen, Düsseldorf
Kunstsammlung Thomas Schmidheiny
Wolfgang Laib
Leopold Museum—Private foundation, Vienna
Louisiana Museum of Modern Art, Humlebæk, Denmark
Musée d'Orsay, Paris
Musée départemental d'art contemporain de Rochechouart
Musée national d'art moderne/Centre de création industrielle, Centre Georges Pompidou, Paris
Musée Picasso, Paris
Museum der Kulturen, Basle
Museum Jean Tinguely, Basle
Museum Ludwig, Sammlung Ludwig, Cologne
Galerie Nelson, Paris
Öffentliche Kunstsammlung Basel, Kunstmuseum and Kupferstichkabinett
Vienna, Österreichische Galerie Belvedere
Orange County Museum of Art
Philadelphia Museum of Art
Collection Anne-Marie and Marc Robelin
Saarland Museum Saarbrücken, Stiftung Saarländischer Kulturbesitz
Sammlung Froehlich, Stuttgart
Stiftung Hans Arp und Sophie Taeuber-Arp e.V.
Staatliche Kunsthalle Karlsruhe
Staatliche Museen zu Berlin, Nationalgalerie, Berlin
Staatsgalerie Stuttgart
Sammlung T, Switzerland
Tate Gallery, London
Van Gogh Museum (Vincent van Gogh Foundation), Amsterdam
Wadsworth Atheneum, Hartford, Connecticut
Wilhelm-Lehmbruck-Museum, Duisburg

as well as the many lenders who wish to remain anonymous.

Contents

Foreword

Trees have always exercised magical powers over man. Artists have often identified with trees, lending them unique characters in their works, finding means of expressing their personalities. We are grateful to all of the lenders, collectors, museums and artists who have made it possible for us to exhibit this selection of outstanding works. Tree depictions of the modern period from its very beginnings until today—works by Caspar David Friedrich and Camille Corot, by Vincent van Gogh, Paul Cézanne, Ferdinand Hodler, Piet Mondrian, Pablo Picasso, Henri Matisse and Paul Klee, by artists of the present—constitute a major portion of the exhibition. We are especially grateful to the artists who contributed to the exhibition with their installations. Also on display is a selection of wooden sculptures created by artists of Africa and the South Seas to lend expression to their concepts of religion, magic and spiritual invocation.

We owe special thanks to Christo and Jeanne-Claude and all of their assistants who, upon their introduction to the park and the museum, enthusiastically agreed to veil over 160 deciduous trees: The entire Berower Park would thus be encircled by a striking wreath of white "cloud sculptures"—the white roof of the museum in its midst. With this achievement they will contribute a further poetic artwork to their world-embracing oeuvre. Their visions—realised on the basis of minutely detailed preparation and precise execution—concoct a unique lyrical magic which, despite the existence of each work for only a few days, implants itself forever in the memory of the viewer.

It is one of the declared intentions of our foundation to link art with life, with existential and essential problems, wherever possible. For this reason we are immensely pleased to introduce two great projects—carried out by the World Wide Fund for Nature and Greenpeace—together for the first time within the framework of our exhibition. With the consent of the Brazilian government and the authorities of the respective regions, the WWF and Greenpeace will safeguard large areas of the rain forest in Amazonia, thus saving them from impending destruction. A report on this project is available in a separate catalogue.

It is our hope that the selected works will render this exhibition a Gesamtkunstwerk, but also that it will heighten our awareness of the gifts trees give us, of how they protect us, of our obligation to provide them with very special protection, not only in faraway lands but here at home as well. We, the world's greatest producers of combustion gasses, should be alarmed, should take precautions.

We hereby gratefully acknowledge the contributions of all who have assisted in the realisation of this exhibition—offering their advice, publishing the catalogue, setting up the installations—and particularly the great efforts of the exhibition team which succeeded in acquiring the many loans within a short period of time. Finally, we would like to express our very special thanks to Reinhold Hohl, Christian Kaufmann and Bernhard Gardi for their introductory texts.

Ernst Beyeler

An Essay by Reinhold Hohl

Pictures About Trees

for Franz Meyer

In the year of Guernica 1937, Bert Brecht wrote the poem *An die Nachgeborenen*
(to the after-born), beginning with the line:
Indeed: I live in dark times!
and containing the following bitter verse:
What times are these, in which
a conversation about trees is all but a crime
Because it includes silence about so many atrocities!

We are the after-born. We are talking here about trees. It is not as though the times were any less dark. On the contrary: They are such that, today, silence about trees is "all but a crime." *Baumzeit* (time of trees) is the title Verena Eggmann and Bernd Steiner gave their encyclopaedic book about historical myths and miracles of trees and the atrocities presently being committed against trees all over the world.[1]

As far as trees are concerned, the times we live in are not only dark but dangerous, at least for those who have joined the "ecological guerilla" (as they call themselves). For example Julia Butterfly Hill, who has lived since December 10, 1997 on a wooden platform sixty metres above the ground in a more than one-thousand-year-old *Sequoia Californiana*. She does not intend to leave this abode in the Headwater Forest of the Redwood Reservation (Humboldt County, California) until the concession to fell this mammoth tree has expired (which will be the case in three years) or until the Pacific Lumber Company abandons its plan. As these words go into print, we have no news of any development in this matter. We live in dark times for trees.

In those dark pre-war times in which Brecht, living in exile in Svendborg, Denmark, wrote the above-quoted poem, the many atrocities also included the events of the Spanish Civil War, particularly the concealment of the truth about the destruction of the Basque city of Guernica. As is well-known, Picasso chose these occurences as the subject of his *Guernica*, a painting containing an often overseen allusion to a tree: The right hand of the broken plaster warrior at the lower edge of the picture holds not only the hilt of a sword but a tender branch as well. A young tree: a new specimen of "Guernikako arbola," the oak of Guernica regarded by the Basques as sacred, the object by which the Spanish kings swore to respect the Basque Provinces' historical right to self-government. The very first newspaper report concerning the outrageous acts committed in Guernica the previous day, telegraphed by the reporter George L. Steer to the *Times* from Bilbao on April 27, 1937, contained a reference to this tree: "The whole town of Guernica was soon in flames except the historic Casa de Juntas . . . where the ancient Basque Parliament used to sit. The famous oak of Guernica, the dried old stump of 600 years and the new shoots of this century, was also untouched."

Today, sixty years later, the branchlet of Picasso's painting has grown into a handsome tree. It stands next to the historical tree stump of Guernica in the midst of a circular colonnade with classicist entablatures, as in a temple, still revered as a political symbol and legacy. And the political consciousness of the Basques is still associated with the hymn to the tree of Guernica: *Guernikako arbola*. In both the Old World and the New, numerous such venerable tree stumps forbid the suppression of historical deeds and misdeeds. Christian wayside chapels have been built around many of Europe's tree relics. A neo-Greek temple like the one in Guernica is inappropriate for the pre-

sent. An artwork like Jean Tinguely's *The Bear of Bursinel* (1990, ill. 1) is a much more fitting expression of our times as a "time of trees": a tree stump like a cruelly mishandled human torso in the clutch of the machine parts and transmissions which served as the instruments of torture.

We are speaking here of trees as they are presented by the paintings and sculptures of this exhibition–i.e. of artworks: We are speaking above all of artworks. Not because they are more important than trees, but because great art encompasses the two most important aspects of what trees mean to man. On the one hand–to summarise–the aspect of the wholly different, the wonderful; on the other hand something man's very own, the aspect of identification with the vicissitudes of existence.

That is what Paul Valéry expressed in *A Dialogue about Trees*, 1944, when he wrote: "The tree and love: in our minds the two can unite to become one idea. Each grows from an imperceptible germ, becomes stronger, expands, branches out; but to the same extent that it reaches skyward (or 'blissward'), it must become rooted in a sphere invisible to us: in our very being."

Ill. 1
Jean Tinguely, *The Bear of Bursinel*, 1990
(see Plate p. 111)

One can hardly imagine a greater contrast to Tinguely's tree sculpture than the painting *The Almond Tree in Bloom* (1946/47, ill. 2) by Pierre Bonnard. As an old man, Bonnard saw the tree flowering outside his window year after year, and nearly every year he recorded the magnificent array of blossoms as though seeing it for the first time. We are reminded of Alberto Giacometti, regarding the acacias in the Rue d'Alésia as he enters a café with James Lord, and saying to himself: "'I've never seen them like that before,' he murmured. Inside the café, when we were seated at the table, he said again: 'I've never seen them like that before.'"

A much different story, incidentally, is told of Piet Mondrian: He is said to have always sat in cafés with his back to the window so as not to see the green of the trees. We will take a thorough look below at Giacometti's and Mondrian's depictions of trees.

To return to Bonnard, in the spring of 1946 he once again began to paint the blossoming almond tree in his garden. It was to be his last painting, and he did not finish it until January of 1947, when his strength had all but waned. He is reported to have said to Charles Terrasse: "'This green on the little spot of earth here at the lower left isn't right; it should be yellow,' and he asked me to help him apply the yellow–or rather the gold."[2]

Ill. 2
Pierre Bonnard, *The Almond Tree in Bloom*, 1946/47
(see Plate p. 75)

This anecdote contains everything which underlies works of art depicting trees: The basic impulse for the painting of the motif arises from the experience, from the excitement and from discoveries of and insights into the meaning of the motif–but in the end it is the work of art which is to emerge and endure. In the case of Bonnard's *Almond Tree in Bloom*, this evaluation is especially justified. We know that it was the last work to be completed before his death. Thus it seems natural to associate the motif of the almond tree, flowering anew every spring, with that of the "tree of life" as it recurs frequently in the cultures of the world, and with the coming death of the artist. He still aspires to counter his death with that which has been his life until that moment, and that which will guarantee his afterlife: a work of art.

It is pointless to ask whether an artwork can stand comparison to a magnificent tree. The painters themselves would probably say no–that is why they continue to paint tree pictures, and their intention in doing so is something other than the imitation of one tree or another. Sculptors and construction artists, for their part, apply the greatest circumspection to the problem of finding a location for their works in parks: the proximity of trees can mean devastating competition. They prefer to stick to large open spaces, far from any trees (– alternatively, they wrap up the trees).

And yet–with the steel construction *Leaves and Tripod* (ca. 1939, plate p. 102)–an artist like Alexander Calder succeeded in evoking the subtlest movements of bobbing branches and the last remaining wind-shaken leaves before their autumnal fall, or–with *The Tree* (1966, plate p. 103)–in depicting the imposing majesty of a tree trunk, its roots grasping the surrounding earth, its masses of foliage in rhythmic motion. Such artworks teach us to discover–or rediscover–the phenomena of nature. The funny thing about Calder's constructions, however, is that their statics and balance are derived from the lever law of the Roman express scale, and have nothing whatever to do with the natural forces responsible for keeping the boughs and branches of trees in a horizontal position as they stretch outward into space. Consider an old apple tree with widely extending horizontal limbs–which, indeed, require support when they are very aged (proving that unsupported natural forces were in effect previously)–and which, in turn, bear boughs, branches, sprigs and, in autumn, an abundance of fruit: We cannot cease to be amazed by the biological and structural powers of trees.

The artists are and were amazed as well. It is unlikely that any modern painter was more amazed than Piet Mondrian. Yet as we will see below, behind these biological forces and beyond the natural statics of his tree depictions (ill. 3, plates pp. 48, 49) he expressed a more universal force: a world order, a universal maxim, exceeding the motif of the tree and the green of nature.

The seventeenth century was the great epoch of the depiction of trees. In the realistic landscape paintings of an artist like Jacob van Ruisdael and the idealistic nature compositions of one like Claude Lorrain, splendid trees demonstrate the existence and force of nature: The one artist offset their position in the picture's rectangle with massive clouds, the other with zones of light.

Ill. 3
Piet Mondrian,
Red Tree, 1908
(see Plate p. 47)

Ill. 4
Egon Schiele, *Autumn Tree in a Breeze, "Autumn Tree" (III),* also *"Winter Tree",* 1912
(see Plate p. 59)

The paintings of both provide evidence of the fact that, to their painters, a tree is more than just a tree. It is a symbol of the comprehensiveness of divine creation, of which he, the individual, is a part, a particle. This point of view no longer applies to the period following the Napoleonic Wars, the age known as "Romantic" and "Biedermeier," characterised by retreat to the solitary individual who, at the very most, longs for integration into an all-encompassing whole. This is the vision echoed in Caspar David Friedrich's *Oak Tree in the Snow* of 1829 (frontispiece p. 6). The aged hero, exposed to the harshness of winter, is a representation of the artist's spiritual consciousness and, to the same degree, an expression of the faithful hope of being sheltered in nature's wholeness. To what extent is this true of modern depictions of trees?

Egon Schiele's *Autumn Tree in a Breeze* (1912, ill. 4)–a work borne by the symbolism of Art Nouveau and influenced by the Expressionist style—may provide an answer applicable to the period and style of its origin. The defoliated tree with its frail trunk, limewashed a bony white, is still anchored in the earthly realm by its roots (although the hill on which it stands is quite reminiscent of a grave mound). But the lateral branch reaching out to the right seeks a precarious balance, and the limbs and branches grasping upward like the skeletons of arms and fingers find no comfort in the nature-wholeness of the heavenly sphere. On the contrary: Schiele's autumn tree performs a dance of death.

We are pulled back to life by the apple tree in Gustav Klimt's painting *Apple Tree II* (ca. 1916, plate p. 57), resplendent with bulging fruits across the entire breadth of the canvas. The apples do not hang between the leaves of the branches as in nature, but are affixed in so decorative a manner that they demand interpretation as symbols of fertility—and the tree as an ornament of life. While viewing this tree portrait it is again important to keep in mind the time and the style in which it was painted, and of the stir caused a few years earlier—at the 1904 Sezession Exhibition of Vienna—by Klimt's only slightly older contemporary Ferdinand Hodler.

III. 5
Ferdinand Hodler,
The Nut Tree, 1907
(see Plate p. 62)

In his youth and in his mature period, Ferdinand Hodler painted trees again and again—so regularly and numerously that his life history might be read in the chronological sequence of his tree pictures. Is it going too far to compare his portraits of trees with self-portraits? They do not reproduce states of mind, as do the tree depictions of—for example—Caspar David Friedrich, but are expressions of a will to be independent, strong and prolific. One of the Ferdinand Hodler paintings exhibited here shows a group of apple trees whose trunks lean toward one another, their fruit-bearing crowns joining to form a single mass (*Apple Trees*, 1897, plate p. 62). The work was made in 1897. We will not allow ourselves a biographical interpretation, however, but rather, from this perspective, turn our gaze temporarily to Samuel Buri's *Apple Power* (1979, plate p. 109): the work of a painter who (like Roy Lichtenstein) chose paintings of his great predecessors (such as Cuno Amiet's *Apple Harvest*, 1907, plate p. 67) as subjects of his own works. Hodler otherwise preferred to paint a single tree, lining up its trunk, the divisions of its branchwork and its crown of leaves or blossoms with the vertical axis of the picture. He thus undoubtedly lent it the individuality of a personality, but in this way he also assigned the tree a supernumerary part in his pictorial composition, his pre-established decision concerning the division of the canvas surface. In later works he—like Mondrian!—weaves the subject into a universal context; his *Nut Tree* of 1907 (ill. 5) stands beneath the vault of heaven, cosmically enveloped by a quasi-symmetrical arrangement of clouds.

Hodler's *Woodcutter* (1910, plate p. 61) surprises us with a counterstatement. Of the four young stems, one must fall; an ominously glowing cloud proclaims the day of judgment. The hour has come for which the trees were planted—utilisation as "pole wood," a cultivated product of the Swiss sustain-yield method of forestry and a suitable motif for a currency note designed by Ferdinand Hodler. Hodler was at the height of his fame, and if we were to seek another self-depiction in this painting, we might well find it in the strength of the woodcutter and the downright excessive impact of his felling act. (This, incidentally, would be a trivial interpretation compared with the tremendous power of the composition.)

Trees as the depiction of one's own potency: That is what Picasso once made of them. Picasso did not often paint trees, and never for *their* own, always for *his* own sake. (We will take a closer look at the tree motifs of early Cubism below, in connection with Cézanne.)

While he was courting the young Françoise Gilot during the Parisian war years of 1943–44, Picasso painted a group of water-colours and oils with the ambiguous title *Vert-Galant* (1943, ill. 6).

This is the name of a little square at the tip of the Ile de la Cité (nearly opposite his residence in the Rue des Grands-Augustins), where trees and benches encircle a statue of King Henry IV, where children play in the afternoon and kisses are exchanged in the night. On the other hand, it means something like "the lustful philanderer," the affectionate nickname under which the legendarily virile Henry IV went down in French history. Even if Picasso's "Vert-Galant" pictures are regarded as mere vedutas of Paris, the biographical context suggests that in their trees—greener than green, brimming with sap—an allusion to something else, something more, is to be found.

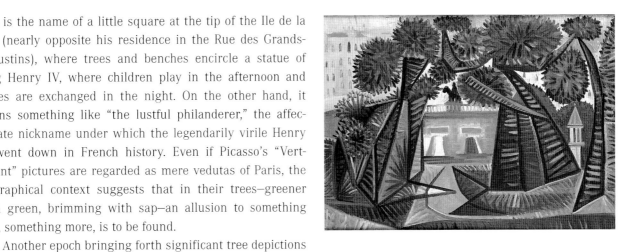

Ill. 6
Pablo Picasso,
Vert-Galant, 1943
(see Plate p. 84)

Another epoch bringing forth significant tree depictions were the years 1961/62, when Picasso produced twenty-seven painted variations on Manet's *Le déjeuner sur l'herbe*, accompanied by a great number of drawings. The focus of his interest in this painting is the composition as a whole and the piquancy of the two female nudes accompanied by two clothed gentlemen exercising philosophical restraint. As the Picasso series progresses, Manet's frame-forming trees take on increasing significance, a circumstance for which an explanation is provided by the painting of the Louisiana Museum (plate p. 85). Here the gentleman on the right sits directly in front of a tree trunk and is Picasso himself, the old man with the palette who "is no longer capable with anything but a paintbrush".[3] He has become one with the tree—to such an extent that he appears to have been carved in its bark. The old Picasso identifies with the old tree, now only a witness of, no longer a participant in the amorous picnic.

Anselm Kiefer painted a virtually heraldic self-identification with a tree trunk in *Tree with Palette* (1978, plate p. 107). The bark of the tree has been so precisely executed that its identification as a pine (in German: Kiefer) cannot be doubted, and the palette affixed to it is the artist's professional symbol—like the indented brass basin formerly hung over the door of a barber's shop. An act of self-representation can also be assumed in Georg Baselitz's *Tree* (1966, ill. 7), dating back to the years when he—a strong but vulnerable young man—began his painting career. In a scene of his play *Wozzeck* (1836), where two women admire a drum major marching past their window, Georg Büchner put the correlation into words: "What a man—like a tree!"

Ill. 7
Georg Baselitz,
The Tree, 1966
(see Plate p. 104)

The underlying principle of the examples discussed above is still fundamentally the tree as the "tree of life," which is its primary symbolic import in Medieval art—as the schematised representation of life in faith and the promise of afterlife. As we have seen, however, this symbolism alludes above all to the figure of the painter and anticipates the death of the tree. What remains to human beings but to associate their own rise and fall with the flourishing and expiration of trees, when we owe the very air we breathe (our "breath of life") to their health, and when the death of the forests means our own suffocation? When we hear the word "Verdun" we remember not only the fallen soldiers of the First World War; in our mind's eye we also see forests shelled to shreds. Even we, the after-born, are still familiar with the field name of that so hotly contested wooded area "Chemin des Dames."

Max Ernst was haunted by his memories of Verdun for a long time and *The Large Forest* (1927, plate p. 88) is only one of the many paintings with which he lamented that act of destruction. Ernst had a special relationship to wood; its bizarre splinters inspired his surrealist paint-

III. 8
Max Ernst, *The Fascina-
tion of the Cypress,
1939* (see Plate p. 89)

ings (*The Fascination of the Cypress*, 1939, ill. 8), and he owed
the effects of the rubbing technique to the rich imagery of
its grain.

Our survey confronts us with yet another contrast
(– the subject of "Trees in Modern Art" is, to be sure, a "wide
field" –) when we turn to the jungle pictures of Henri
Rousseau. The events taking place in our example of the year
1905 are perhaps no less violent: *The Hungry Lion Attacking
an Antelope* is the title (plate p. 37), further elucidated by the
artist in the exhibition catalogue as follows: "The hungry lion
hurls himself upon the antelope and tears it to pieces; the
panther anxiously awaits the moment when he will get his
share. Shedding tears, the birds of prey have hacked a piece
of flesh from the back of the poor animal." Yet the jungle setting is a botanist's paradise, a healthy
environment bursting with vitality, every bough, every branch, every leaf a splendid sample of its
species and genus—as I said, a paradise. And if the brutality to which the jungle subjects humans
and animals could be suppressed, it would be (and would have been for the painter) an ideal paradise. With these pictures, the burgeoning twentieth century provided a sobering but truthful
sequel to the paradisaic visions of the early seventeenth century (as painted, for example, by Jan
Brueghel or Roelant Savery). Never again will we walk in Goethe's footsteps to the Ettersberg and
stroll without horror through the beech forest there bearing the name *Buchenwald*.

On the other hand, the city dweller will be afforded a carefree experience of the woods in
Jean Dubuffet's "Hourloupe" constructions such as *The Forest* (1969) or *The Group of Trees* (1969,
plate p. 99) if ever the models of ramose tree groups are constructed at a height of ten to fifteen
metres, as called for by the plans. The dying forest syndrome must not be feared, for the trees will
be made of synthetic material. The advantages of such a construction have been undergoing a test
for over twenty years in Manhattan, where a large Dubuffet tree was erected on the Chase
Manhattan Plaza (in place of the originally planned *Large Standing Woman* by Giacometti, to be
discussed below) and where the vestiges of air pollution and acid rain are simply sprayed off with
a hose. Nobody seems to know what measures will someday be required for the work's environ-
mentally safe disposal. But, be that as it may, it is worthwhile considering why a tree was chosen
as a motif for the decoration of this urban space. (Today trees have been planted along many of the
streets of New York. On 22nd Street, in front of the DIA Center for the Arts, are three of the 7,000
oaks, complete with their basalt columns, which Joseph Beuys commissioned all urbanites to
plant.) Is the sculpture at the foot of the skyscraper in the Wall Street district to be understood as
a "Memorial to the Unknown Tree"? Or as a daily reminder of the fact that there are not only
shops, and not only business transactions, but also such things as trees and works of art? Seen on
site, Dubuffet's tree is like a loyal companion, sharing the rat race of life with us during our lunch
breaks.

To the lonely van Gogh, trees were also friends and companions. As he once wrote to his
brother, when he worked out-of-doors he drew and painted trees as though they were human
figures. Is this not unmistakably true of the picture of an old tree stump, sprouting—how wonderful!—new branches (*The Old Yew Tree*, 1888, plate p. 28)? In *The Sower* (1888, plate p. 26) a large
tree trunk (following the compositional example of Japanese woodcuts) leans toward the farmer as
he sows the endless plains, utterly alone in the world. The disk of light above his head shines like
a halo; the sprouting branches and leaves herald the germination of his crops.

Van Gogh's blossoming trees and cypresses are also pictures of consolation and friendship.
They show individuals who have suffered good and hard fates of their own—such as the storm-
tested nut pines in *Pine Trees Against an Evening Sky* (1889, plate p. 29)—and share his, giving

him courage and faith. Yet the rows of trees along the ancient burial road of Les Alyscamps in Arles (*The Alyscamps, Avenue in Arles*, 1888, ill. 9) are more than that. They line and protect the avenue leading from the turbulent foreground to the churchyard in the back, an allegory of the path of life. These contents are so powerful that the spatial perspective constructed by means of the tree rows seems a trivial detail in comparison. The orange-yellow of the leaves shines like the gold of an altarpiece. Somehow similar, somehow different is the effect of the trees, depicted in rows or singly, in the works of Edvard Munch. Unlike van Gogh, Munch often arranges his trees and tree groups on planes parallel to the picture surface. Like staggered walls they divide the picture into zones, contributing their oppressive effect to the message conveyed by the work's motif. The spiritual distress emanated by works such as *Children in the Forest* (1903) or *The Red House in the Snow* (1925/26, plate p. 54), a depiction of the artist's residence, is immediately sensed by the observer. Munch's pictures of trees serve the expression of haunting sensations which dissolve and disperse in the friendly clouds of the sky. The tree images of Chaim Soutine emit an even stronger feeling of personal misery. *The Tree of Vence* (ca. 1929, plate p. 71) is a virtual self-portrait of this victim of life's hardships. But enough psychology!

III. 9
Vincent van Gogh,
The Alyscamps, Avenue in Arles, 1888
(see Plate p. 27)

Two other paintings by the same artist provide a much different perspective on the depiction of the tree in modern art. Their titles alone—*Poplars, Civry* (ca. 1939, ill. 10) and *Large Poplars in Civry* (1939/40, plate p. 73) signify to the art historian that these works are concerned with more than expressive self-depiction in the form of a tree. They are reflections of both the art of van Gogh as well as the series of poplar paintings produced by Monet forty years earlier in Giverny (or places near Giverny), including *Poplars on the Banks of the Epte, Twilight* (1891, ill. 11) and *Poplars on the Banks of the Epte. White and Yellow Accents* (1891, plate p. 25). This group of altogether four pictures is one more indication of the fact that art, while it may be inspired by deep sensations, elevated thoughts and lively statements of and about itself, owes its state of being-what-it-is-and-nothing-else to previous artworks. One is more likely to read Soutine's nervous (or should we say neurotic?) personality in his depictions of poplars than to undertake their ranking in comparison with the works of Monet. But for the purposes of examining the significance of trees in modern art, Monet's paintings are the more important documents.

III. 10
Chaim Soutine,
Poplars, Civry, ca. 1939
(see Plate p. 72)

To an even greater extent than Monet's landscapes of the pioneering years of Impressionism (1872–1876), these works mark the advancement to that which we call "modern art." Claude Monet did not paint his series of poplars—or of coastal cliffs, haystacks, Norwegian snow fields and subtropical gardens on the Côte d'Azure—to provide views of the respective subject, thereby expressing their eternal integration in nature. His intention was to use the various pigments and linseed oil on the canvas in front of him to reproduce momentary phenomena of light and colour—changing canvasses every hour, if that was what the sun's position demanded. "Twilight" and "white and yellow accents" are the real motifs of the two poplar works by Claude Monet exhibited here. Nor will the observer fail to notice the way in which the poplar rows and their reflections in the water lend rhythm to the composition and spatial depth to the canvas.

The degree to which Monet thus founded the modern pictorial concept (as Cézanne did as well, if in a different way) can best be seen by reverting our attention to nineteenth-century landscape paintings containing trees. In the final analysis, Corot's *Italian Villa Behind Pines* (ca. 1860, plate p. 23) is still an idealised veduta, its

trees expressing the concept of eternity—as in Claude Lorrain's idealising compositions of the Roman Campagna. With regard to its depiction of the tree and the weather, Courbet's realistic painting *The Gust of Wind* (ca. 1855) can compete with a Jacob van Ruisdael, even if it fails to be inspired by a belief in heavenly compensation for the tree's perils (or the human being's, or the painter Courbet's). With Monet, all psychological and philosophical identification ceases. A tree is no longer a tree, but in its optical appearance here and now a painting process—and thus all the more wonderful.

What about Cézanne? His landscape paintings are naturally full of tree groups, and he often drew or painted single trees on the wayside, depicting them as unique individuals. An example is seen in the water-colour painting *Road with Trees on a Slope* (ca. 1904, plate p. 34). Cézanne is known to have said that when he painted outdoors an Almighty Father revealed himself to him—but he tells us no more. His paintings are not pictures about trees but pictures containing trees, compositions thanks to the trees.

The art historian John Rewald identified Cezánne's landscape motifs on location and was thus able to give the paintings more exact titles. A work previously known as *View of the Sea at L'Estaque*, for example, he renamed *Boulders, Pine Trees and Sea at l'Estaque* (1883–1885, ill. 12). The painting's two protagonists, the boulder and the tree trunk curved against its side in the centre of the picture, thus receive the attention they deserve. Together they are a pair of counterparts: dry, hard, rigid, dead mass vs. lush, vulnerable, growing, living line. Gravestone vs. tree of life? Is this all too humanly oriented interpretation really the subject matter of the depiction? In my view: no. In Cézanne's work, each and every brushstroke on the canvas is the subject matter of the picture, in other words the equivalent on the flat canvas of a phenomenon seen in the shimmering distance. Here—more than in the work of any other modern painter—the content of the artwork is the artwork itself. We are not looking at trees which Cézanne *saw*, even if that is the first impression his landscape paintings make on us and this first impression is substantiated by photographic evidence. Rather, we see the trees Cézanne *painted*. This naturally applies to all paintings with trees in them; nevertheless, there is a difference between these and traditional depictions of trees. The pine trees in Corot's *Italian Villa Behind Pines*, for example, remind everyone who has travelled through Italy of trees he has seen in the Campagna di Roma; they tell him as much, so to speak, in Latin: "Haec est Italia, diis sacra" ("This

is Italy, a land sacred to the gods"). That is the theme of Corot's picture. The theme of Cézanne's picture is the translation of the trees into a work of art (as he expressed it: "réaliser": the lending of reality to the trees). For Cézanne, trees are servants to his compositions.

In *The Bridge of Maincy* (1879/80, plate p. 31)—a masterpiece comparable only to compositions by Poussin, for example his *Saint Peter and Saint John Healing a Lame Man* (1655, Metropolitan Museum, New York)—the tree group to the right shoots straight upward in order to complement the diagonal, the horizontal and the circular elements of the bridge, and vice versa. And—as is naturally the case with every tree in Cézanne's landscape paintings—the tree trunk in the left half of the picture stands exactly where the artist wanted it, where the composition needed it. And yet nobody would say that Cézanne's depictions of trees have something artificial about them. Too perceptible are the hot wind of the Provence and the cool shadows of the pines!

The autonomy of the artwork, the sovereignty of the painter with regard to the motif, the inherent laws of painting: These are the

aspects noticed by both the "Matissites" (Henri Matisse, André Derain and others, originally including Braque) and the "Picassites" (Pablo Picasso, later joined by Georges Braque and Derain) in the memorial exhibition following Cézanne's death in 1906. Braque (see *Landscape at l'Estaque*, 1906, plate p. 38) and Derain (see *Landscape at l'Estaque*, 1907, plate p. 39) visited the place so that the "genius loci" would endow them with Cézanne's genius. In 1908 Matisse and Picasso also painted several Cézanne-like landscape views with trees, the former for example *View of Collioure* (Metropolitan Museum, New York), the latter *Landscape, La Rue-des-Bois* (1908, ill. 13). In the later work of both artists, leaf and tree motifs are nothing more than impulses for artistic aspiration, the one aiming towards harmony of colour tones and the arabesques of the silhouette, the other towards the virtuality of bodies in space and the ambiguity of spatial interrelationships–trees or no trees.

The treetop in Picasso's *Tree* (1907, plate p. 40) has nothing whatever to do with botany. The curves and surface segments may be "realised" branches and foliage–who knows?–but above all, with their contradictory confusion of light and shadow, they comprise and create pictorial space without perspective and corporeality without substance. In early Cubism, beginning in 1908, Picasso and Braque placed the inconsistently foreshortened and shaded natural motifs in the service of their intention to fold the canvas surface "forward" and "backward" and yet to keep it flat–thus cancelling the illusionism of painting with illusions of illusions. The steps in the terrain and the trunks of the trees in Picasso's *Landscape, La Rue-des-Bois* possess volume and location–and yet they possess neither. The picture-book quality of the oversize tree leaves comes from Picasso's encounter with Henri Rousseau (see plate p. 37).[4] If the remotest inkling of tree magic can be determined in Braque's and Picasso's later Cubist works, then only between 1912 and 1914 in the "faux bois" of the glued-on or imitated cutouts of wallpaper printed with wood-grain designs.

The manner in which tree depictions remain a theme in the works of artists associated with Cubism can be seen in paintings of Fernand Léger after 1910. In his forest pictures, tree trunks and branches become pipes and pipe fragments; where trees add green to a cityscape, their crowns are smoke-balls of colour which flatten to discs in later works.

The importance of Cézanne's leadership along this path is expressed in the very title of Léger's *Level Crossing* (*Le Passage à niveau*, 1912, plate p. 43), a play on words. On the one hand, it simply names the subject of the picture, the ground-level intersection of a country road and a railroad line, protected by a lattice gate. But it also alludes to Cézanne's personal term "passages"

(transitions), which comprises one of the secrets of his art: the virtually imperceptible transitions from one plane of pictorial depth to the next deeper plane, generated by a tonal nuance within a single brushstroke, or the spatial jumps negated by colour and brushstroke, creating a continuous pictorial space in which the painting surface is consistently respected. The same phenomenon occurs in Léger's painting, where the disc fragments representing crowns of trees are the vehicles for achieving "flat pictorial depth." Of course Léger's painting shows us a landscape with trees, houses, telephone poles (their decreasing height serving to construct the spatial perspective), an approaching locomotive to the left ... but all as though in a picture puzzle where one cannot see the forest for the trees. In 1913/14 Léger composes non-objective paintings from these disc-like elements, giving them titles such as *Still Life with Multi-Coloured Cylinders* or *Contrast of Forms* (of which there are examples in the Fondation Beyeler), later *Mechanical Parts*. What used to be a tree becomes a mechanical component, even later a traffic notice in the urban forest of signs.

The most important artistic development in modern painting, Cubism, would thus prove to be the wrong track for our art historical tour of the forest, if an impressive series (plates pp. 47–49, 51) did not point the way to Mondrian's abstract compositions.

Piet Mondrian regarded trees with religious devotion. Or to be more specific, with theosophical mysticism. He saw them and all of nature as superficial manifestations of an invisible, realer reality. The aim of his painting was to provide insight into this true existence. His use of tree images to approach this goal—and with it non-objective art—in the years from 1908 to 1913 has become a classic demonstration of the history of modern art.

These paintings were always concerned with a single tree—either a widely reaching apple tree or a towering eucalyptus—whose trunk corresponded directly with the axis of the picture. The aim of the works was to depict the forces rising out of the horizontally sprawling, moist-warm and fertile earth through trunk, limbs and branches to partake of the spirituality of the vertical and become transfigured in the cool altitudes of the heavens. We might regard *Red Tree* (1908, plate p. 47) as the beginning of the series; its coloration reveals the Symbolist-Fauvist origins of the idea. From 1910 to 1913, the decisive influence on the pictorial development was Cubism. This is mirrored in the subdued shades of ochre and grey and in the pre-eminence of linear construction, serving an illusorily illusionist means of depicting three-dimensional bodies and space which never stray from the surface of the canvas. Here art responded to the tradition of copying nature with a form of depiction that was intellectual in the work of Picasso and Braque, spiritual in the work of Mondrian (*Eucalyptus*, 1912, ill. 14). And one year later the autonomy of the artwork with respect to the tree motif is so great that Mondrian now entitles the paintings "compositions," the tree mentioned only parenthetically at best, as an indication of the picture's subject (*Composition No. XVI [Composition I, Trees]*, 1912/13, plate p. 51). After Mondrian banned curved lines, diagonals and secondary colours from his paintings in 1914, from then on regarding horizontal and vertical lines, black, white and the primary colours as the only valid pictorial elements, we can no longer discern natural depictions in his works, even if his geometric compositions are nothing other than glimpses into a truer, supranatural nature.

If at this point we friends of the magic of trees feel abandoned by modern art, we may be pleased to discover witty, often enigmatic tree portrayals in the subtle, charming pictures of artists like Paul Klee (plates pp. 81–83) or René Magritte (plates pp. 86 and 87). As a myth, a tree of life, a tree of the universe, the tree symbol would have no place in the great art of our time—if not for "Vladimir" and "Estragon": Beckett and Giacometti.

Alberto Giacometti is not known for his tree motifs but rather for portraits and busts, and above all for his greatly attenuated female figures. Yet the intention here is to point out that the idea underlying these figures—not least of all the never-realised project of a *Large Standing Woman* (ill. 15) on the Chase Manhattan Plaza of New York—is a real tree legend.

In 1949 Giacometti made a series of unusual coloured pencil drawings in which a human figure as thin as a rod stands next to a huge tree (*Figure Beneath a Tree*, 1949, ill. 16) or a man's head in the lower half of the picture looks into the crown of a tree high above him. The motif must have had personal significance for the artist, for as long as he was alive these drawings were solely in the possession of his family and friends. He later repeated the depiction, but in the manner of a reminiscence (*Man and Tree*, 1962).

The memory may go back to Giacometti's childhood. A letter he wrote in 1950 to his art dealer Pierre Matisse contains a passage about the *The Glade* (plate p. 93) and the *The Forest* (or, much further down in the text: *The Cage*) (plate p. 95):

III. 14
Piet Mondrian,
Eucalyptus, 1912
(see Plate p. 49)

"To my surprise, the *Composition with Nine Figures* [The Glade] seemed to realize the impression I had received when seeing a glade (it was like a pasture grown wild, with trees and shrubs on the edge of a forest) which had greatly intrigued me. I would have liked to paint it, to make something of it but I had left with the feeling that I had lost it. The *Composition with Seven Figures and a head* [The Forest] reminded me of a forest corner seen for many years (that was during my childhood) and where trees with their naked and slender trunks, limbless almost to the top and behind which could be seen granite boulders, had always appeared to me like personages immobilized in the course of their wanderings and talking among themselves."

In these compositions (and in another bearing the title *The Cage*, 1950), the "figures" are motionless, elongated women, the "heads" low male busts. The drawings as well as the bronze compositions referred to by the artist in his letter allude to an enigmatic theme which (as expressed in a second letter to Pierre Matisse) is not designated in a sufficiently general manner by the titles *The Glade* and *The Forest*: "One should be able to think of anything." Let us make a mental note of the comparison of slender female figures with trees, and of tall trees with persons.

In 1953 Giacometti received a commission from America to design door panels for the mausoleum of Edgar J. Kaufmann in Bear Run, Pennsylvania—located on the very estate on which the deceased had had the house "Falling Water" built by Frank Lloyd Wright in 1935. The design consisted of two trees. Whatever they symbolise, Giacometti—who had never seen the site—chooses to have the procession from the wooded estate to the netherworld flanked by trees. Naturally, these are traditional cemetery motifs: trees of life, trees of afterlife.

In 1958 the commission for a sculpture on the Chase Manhattan Plaza in New York followed. Giacometti had no success with the group *Large Standing Woman* (larger than life-size), *Walking Man* (life-size) or *Monumental Head on a Base*, and his final idea was of a single figure of a woman six or seven metres high which would have towered above the businesspeople and their activities—like a tree, we say, remembering the young Giacometti's tree experience and the forest analogies of 1950.

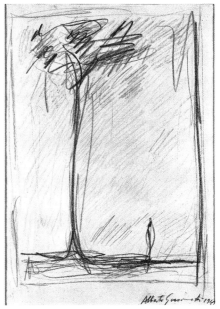

In 1961 Giacometti realised a tree sculpture for a place of much greater significance. "A country road. A tree. Evening" are Samuel Beckett's instructions for the stage setting for *Waiting for Godot* (1948; premier, 1953; production by Jean-Louis Barrault in the Paris Odéon, 1961). There Vladimir and Estragon are waiting for Godot:

Vladimir: *We're waiting for Godot ... He said by the tree ...*

Estragon: *What is it?*

Vladimir: *I don't know. A willow.*

Estragon: *Where are the leaves?*

Vladimir: *It must be dead.*

Estragon: *No more weeping.*

The rendezvous by the tree is a scene of universal significance and, wretched as the stage prop was supposed to be, the poet wanted the now world-famous sculptor to execute the tree. Giacometti recounted the incident to the writer Giorgio Soavi:

"Beckett—he asked me to make the stage set for *Godot*. For this a tree was needed. A tree and the moon. We spent the entire night in the studio in front of a plaster tree, making it sparser, smaller, the branches thinner. It never looked good and neither of us were pleased with it. Both of us kept saying to the other: Maybe like this …"

In Act II the tree has four or five leaves.

Vladimir: *Look at it.*

> They look at the tree.

Estragon: *I see nothing.*

Vladimir: *But yesterday evening it was all black and bare. And now it's covered with leaves … .*

Estragon: *It must be Spring.*

The writer and the sculptor had been expressing themselves to each other on nightly walks since 1937, and Giacometti is likely to have understood the importance of Beckett's tree for the play. His sculpture of wire and plaster rags has not been preserved. Thus the most significant tree depiction in the art of the 20th century remains a legend.

Vladimir: *Everything is dead but the tree … .*

Estragon: *Why don't we hang ourselves?*

Giacometti supplied the answer in the mythical *Large Standing Woman*—the greater-than-life-size figure of a woman, to whom we look up as to a tree.

1   Verena Eggmann und Bernd Steiner, *Baumzeit*, Zurich, Werd Publishing House, 1995; 7th edition 1997.

2   Original text in *La Revue du Louvre*, Paris, 1964, No. 3, p. 144.

3   Original text: "C'est avec mon pinceau que je baise," as Renoir said of himself when painting female nudes.

4   This is also the art historical genealogy of Kasimir Malevich's *Landscape (Winter)*, 1909, plate p. 44.

25 CAMILLE COROT · THE ITALIAN VILLA BEHIND PINES · UNDATED · 61³/₄ x 44³/₄"

84 CLAUDE MONET · POPLARS ON THE BANKS OF THE EPTE, TWILIGHT · 1891 · 40 x 26"

85 CLAUDE MONET · POPLARS ON THE BANKS OF THE EPTE · 1891 · 40 x 26"

44 VINCENT VAN GOGH · THE SOWER · 1888 · 29¹/₄ x 37"

42 VINCENT VAN GOGH · THE OLD YEW TREE · 1888 · 36³/₄ x 29"

19 PAUL CÉZANNE · LANDSCAPE NEAR AIX—THE PLAIN OF THE ARC RIVER · 1892–1895 · 33 x 26¹/₄"

21 PAUL CÉZANNE · ROAD WITH TREES ON A SLOPE · ca. 1904 · 18³/₄ x 12¹/₄"

27 ANDRÉ DERAIN · LANDSCAPE AT L'ESTAQUE · 1907 · 29 x 36¹/₂"

90 **PABLO PICASSO** · THE TREE · SUMMER, 1907 · 37$^1/_2$ x 37$^1/_4$"

81 PIET MONDRIAN · EUCALYPTUS TREE (BLACK) · 1910 · 20^1/$_2$ x 15^1/$_2$"

79 HENRI MATISSE · THE GARDEN AT ISSY (THE STUDIO IN CLAMART) · ca. 1917 · 51 x 35"

88 EDVARD MUNCH · THE RED HOUSE IN THE SNOW · 1925/26 · 27¹/₄ x 36"

87 **EDVARD MUNCH** · WINTER NIGHT · 1900 · 32¹/₄ x 48¹/₄"

69 GUSTAV KLIMT · THE LARGE POPLAR (II), ALSO "RISING STORM" · 1903 · 40 x 40"

70 GUSTAV KLIMT · APPLE TREE II · ca. 1916 · 32 x 32"

95 **EGON SCHIELE** · AUTUMN TREE IN A BREEZE, "AUTUMN TREE" (III), ALSO "WINTER TREE" · 1912 · 32 x 32¹/₄"

57 FERDINAND HODLER · THE FIR TREE (NEAR CHAMBY) · 1905 · 38^1/$_2$ x 26^1/$_2$"

56   FERDINAND HODLER · APPLE TREES · 1897 · 20³/₄ x 15¹/₂"
59   FERDINAND HODLER · THE NUT TREE · 1907 · 29 x 25¹/₂"

58 **FERDINAND HODLER** · CHERRY TREE IN BLOOM · 1905 · 23¹/₂ x 18¹/₂"

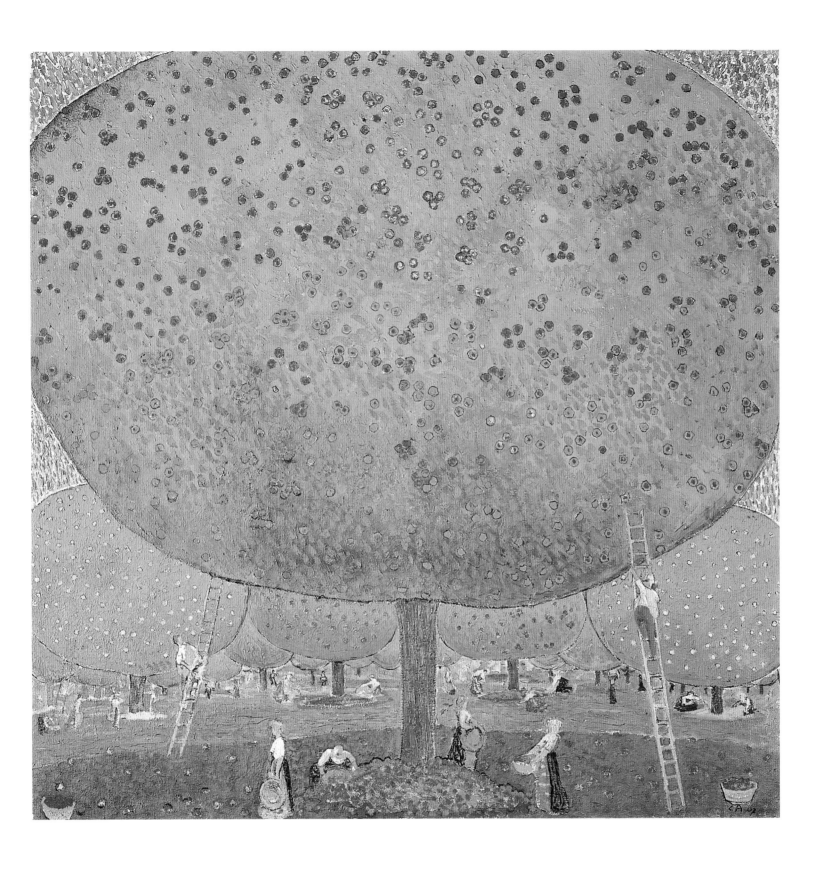

2 **CUNO AMIET** · APPLE HARVEST · 1907 · 40 x 40¹/₄"

1   CUNO AMIET · WINTER LANDSCAPE · 1904 · 21¹/₂ x 25¹/₂"

3 CUNO AMIET · WINTER · 1958 · 39¹/₄ x 36¹/₂"

96 CHAIM SOUTINE · THE TREE OF VENCE · ca. 1929 · 32¹/₂ x 24¹/₂"

98 CHAIM SOUTINE · POPLARS, CIVRY · ca. 1939 · 24¹/₂ x 13¹/₄"

97 CHAIM SOUTINE · LARGE POPLARS IN CIVRY · 1939/40 · 29^1/$_4$ x 21^1/$_2$

86   CLAUDE MONET · WEEPING WILLOW · 1920–1922 · 44 x 40"

11 **PIERRE BONNARD** · THE ALMOND TREE IN BLOOM · 1946/47 · 22 x 15"

62 ERNST LUDWIG KIRCHNER · FEHMARN LANDSCAPE – FOREST PATH · 1914 · 48 x 36"

63 **ERNST LUDWIG KIRCHNER** · MOUNTAIN FOREST · 1918–1920 · 32 x 28"

67 **PAUL KLEE** · FOREST WITCHES · 1938/145 (K5) · 39¹/₂ x 29¹/₂"

92 PABLO PICASSO · VERT-GALANT · JUNE 25, 1943 · 25³/₄ x 36³/₄"

93 PABLO PICASSO · LE DÉJEUNER SUR L'HERBE · 1961 · 52 x 38³/₄"

76 **RENÉ MAGRITTE** · THE WATERFALL · 1961 · 32^1/$_2$ x 40"

30 **MAX ERNST** · THE FASCINATION OF THE CYPRESS · 1939 · 29¹/₂ x 40"

101 WOLS · TREES · ca. 1946 · 32¹/₂ x 26"

34 ALBERTO GIACOMETTI · THE GLADE · 1950 · 22¹/₂ x 23¹/₂ x 19¹/₂"

36 ALBERTO GIACOMETTI · MAN IN A LANDSCAPE · 1958 · 24 x 32¹/₂"

1959 Alberto Giacometti

28 **JEAN DUBUFFET** · THE GROUP OF TREES · MAY 9, 1969 · 38 x 55¹/₂ x 50³/₄"

14 **ALEXANDER CALDER** · LEAVES AND TRIPOD · ca. 1939 · 94¹/₂ x 66"
15 **ALEXANDER CALDER** · THE TREE · 1966 · 208 x 428"

5   GEORG BASELITZ · THE TREE · 1966 · 64³/₄ x 52"

8 GEORG BASELITZ · SHRUBBERY · 1975 · 80 x 64³/₄"

9 **GEORG BASELITZ** · MOTHER OF THE GARLAND · 13. XI. 96 · 12^1/$_2$ x 37^1/$_2$ x 32^1/$_2$"

61 **ANSELM KIEFER** · TREE WITH PALETTE · 1978 · 110¹/₄ x 74³/₄"

13 **SAMUEL BURI** · APPLE POWER · 1979 · 81¹/₄ x 81¹/₄"

99 JEAN TINGUELY · THE BEAR OF BURSINEL · 1990 · 108³/₄ x 77¹/₂ x 88"

Markus Brüderlin

The Last Tree

Perceptions of the Tree in Contemporary Art

What is saved in art is thus forever lost to life. Despite this—or because of it—,
not the pictures portraying nature obtrusively as a sleepy alpine farm or an infinite ring of sunlight,
but rather the art in which, according to Kant, nature has recreated itself (as opposed to illustrating
or imitating itself) may be the place where, following nature's destruction, the last undistorted
memory of the idea of nature will be preserved.

KONRAD PAUL LIESSMANN[1]

Due to the breakneck pace of technological development, the systems in which our lives take place
are dominated increasingly by diffusion and fragmentation. Our experience of nature, if nature
can still be experienced as such, is also subject to this process. For this reason, a presentation of
contemporary art concerned with the subject of the tree can no longer simply exhibit (entire)
trees—trees which by virtue of their form still embody the ideal of oneness and wholeness. The vis-
itor to the large exhibition room on the lower level of the Fondation Beyeler will search in vain for
blossoming trees or trees towering up in the pride of their impressiveness. He will find only
traces, fragments, reconstructions or mechanically finished products of that natural object which
is among Earth's largest living beings: On the floor an eight-metre-large circle formed by interlocking pieces of driftwood; behind that, cut off by the picture frame and turned upside down, a
series of barely recognisable tree stumps; a luminous yellow rectangle like a carpet, encompassed
by a chapel-like spatial compartment (plate p. 123). Even the work on display in the adjacent winter garden—a tree trunk with sawed-off branches—looks like a piece of propped-up nature.

The selection of works in this part of the exhibition is not intended to provide a survey of "the
tree in contemporary art." It might better be described as the realisation of an attempt to bring
together mutually coordinated contemporary perceptions of the phenomenon around which the
entire exhibition revolves, and of aesthetic experiences of nature in general.

Richard Long—Wolfgang Laib—Giuseppe Penone
The search for lost intimacy with nature

The stairway connecting the early modern with the contemporary section of the exhibition not
only represents a spatial interruption but also marks a turning point in art. In the 1960s and 70s,
art underwent a radical renunciation of the traditional media of painting and sculpture. No longer
wanting to limit their art to the canvas square, the makers of so-called Land Art, Process Art and
Arte Povera sought new materials and open fields of expression. And not only that! They also left
the studio and art's traditional space. Some of them went to nature—into the countryside, to work
directly in nature. They were no longer satisfied with simply illustrating it or, like Klee and
Kandinsky, exploring its laws and structures on paper and canvas. They wanted to deal directly
with the objects of nature and develop the techniques and basic forms of their art from the elementary forms and processes of nature.

In 1968 the artist Richard Long, a native of Bristol, left his studio to commence his extended
"walks" in all parts of the world. He marches cross-country along strict geometric formations such
as circles, squares and straight lines which he plots previously on a map. For an eighty-six-mile
hike in 1986 he chose a series of fifteen trees forming a straight path, which he followed consis-

III. 1
Richard Long:
A Circle in Alaska—
Bering Strait Driftwood
on the Arctic Circle,
1977

tently ("From Tree to Tree"). At prominent points along the way where there were no distinct trail marks, the artist created elementary ground sculptures—spirals, rings, circles or lines consisting of natural materials found at the site (ill. 1). By 1970, Long had begun to transfer these sculptures to art's traditional space, the museum.

While the ground sculptures are made primarily of stones of the respective region, many use wood as well, including driftwood found by the artist along stream beds (plate p. 122). Our exhibition presents a circle formed of driftwood, washed into soft shapes by water, and detached pieces of tree bark. This is a construction associated with the idea of mentally reassembling the many trees to which these fragments belonged before being dispersed by wind and weather or carried away by water. The integration of the scattered pieces into a strictly circular shape is an attempt to reconstruct something of the original form of the fragmented tree.

The concentration of that which has been scattered—a similar thing happens in another work of the exhibition. Wolfgang Laib unites a material which nature disseminates in thousands and thousands of places: pollen. In homeopathic doses, the pollen of trees such as the hazelnut or the pine is found on thousands of flower clusters, awaiting distribution in all directions by wind and bees (ill. 2). Arriving before either of them, the artist collected the pollen from the pine trees—not to distribute it, however, but to concentrate it in the exhibition space as a glowing carpet measuring 2.2 x 2.6 metres. In addition to the impressive presence of this piece of condensed nature, it echoes the idea of the exhibition in inspiring the contemplative powers of the viewer, who finds himself trying to imagine the number of trees from which this pollen was taken, and the number which could potentially grow out of it.

In addition to his pollen fields, Wolfgang Laib produces quite different works employing natural materials, such as slightly moulded marble slabs coated with milk. His highly sensitive art has inspired a wide spectrum of interpretations, as an expression of holy-mystical ecstasy in which the individual attains his innermost self[2] for example or, in connection with Buddhism, as the reconciliation of nature and art, finding its sensualisation in the intense synthesis of colour, form and matter. The employment of this fine reproductive and nutritional substance and the meditative concentration to which the auratic pollen rectangle leads can indeed be understood as the search for an elementary experience close to nature. But paradoxically, the search is carried out

III. 2
Wolfgang Laib:
Bog with Pines

under the influence of a formulation extremely remote from nature—autonomous, monochrome painting—and in the emptiness of the neutral exhibition room. Like in the work of Long, the absoluteness of the geometric shape and the purity of the material join to create imagery that permits viewers to reflect on their relationship to nature in an aesthetically more authentic manner than does mere imitation. We are reminded of Adorno's disagreement with Bloch: Nature reveals itself in its very abstraction, denaturalisation and asceticism, and not in the mimesis of the naturally beautiful or in idyllic allegories of conciliation.[3] The high degree of abstraction proves that Laib's concern is not the naive healing of a dichotomous relationship, and certainly not the saving of nature. For, as Konrad Paul Liessman commented in response to the beauty priests of the ecology movement, "What is saved in art is thus forever lost to life."[4]

Whereas we are not shown any actual trees in the work of Richard Long and Wolfgang Laib, in the contribution by the Italian artist Giuseppe Penone we encounter a tree which has been laid out along the longitudinal axis of the winter garden, its branches having been sawed off in a remarkable fashion. Yet this tree is an illusion. In reality we are standing in front of a massive wooden beam. In a toilsome process, Penone reverse-worked a eleven-metre-long construction beam back to an earlier stage of its development, when the beam was a tree (ill. 3). The artist took his orientation from the rings in which the growth of the bark deposited itself year after year in a very much longer process. Layer by layer, the machine-made cubature has been removed with the aid of chisel and plane (plate p. 121).

III. 3
Giuseppe Penone:
*Tree Eleven Metres
Long,* 1980

This sculpturally sensitive credo contradicts the classical pathos of the Artist-Creator, who imposes his forms upon the willing material. Penone perceives himself rather as a "poetic enlightener"[5] who "sounds out" nature in search of its inner powers of life and form, while minutely probing its points of contact to non-nature, i.e. to culture and technology. Thus his aim is not to restore the tree back to its original natural beauty following its assault by the circular saw and the plane, but rather to examine the process of nature's utilisation. By artistically reversing this irreversible process, he demonstrates that nature is not perceivable in its original form, as nature itself, but only through its exploitation—in the Kantian sense, as nature re-formed by human perception.

Rodney Graham—Bill Viola
The tree in the age of its own technical reproducibility

With their direct utilisation of natural materials and their expeditions into landscapes hardly touched by human civilisation, Long, Laib and Penone describe in their works the search for a lost intimacy with nature. Yet unlike the naive invocation of idyllic images, their works demonstrate clearly that art provides access to nature only via detours—if at all—, i.e. via processes of formalisation and abstraction. Compared to this intimacy imagined by means of material realism and formal abstraction, nature appears in the photographic works of Rodney Graham as something utterly domesticated, a piece of culture and a projection surface for human states of mind.

We would have to stand on our heads in front of Rodney Graham's photos of cedars in order to take in the lower segments of mighty tree giants cut out by the picture frame (plate p. 127)—incidentally, a view reminiscent of the Old Germanic conception of monumental trees as visible expressions of the earth's axis. The inversion is not meant to evoke mythical images, however, but to allude to the technique of the camera obscura, the first means of reproducing reality photomechanically. The artist used this optical device to design complex architectural constructions intended for installation directly in front of large trees in public spaces (ill. 4).

The employment of the camera obscura in its original manner calls to mind the change of perception brought about by technical innovations of the early nineteenth century. The statics of the old-fashioned picture-taking device, which corresponds with the statics of a firmly rooted tree, is representative of technology-supported vision from the seventeenth to the nineteenth century. With the invention of photochemistry and the portable camera, everything became mobile, and reality increasingly subjective. The now mobile observer-subject, idealised in the flâneur of early modern art, became autonomous; the visual field was inexorably fragmented through his movement, as clearly demonstrated in the Cubist style of painting. Rodney Graham's upside-down tree portraits therefore do not show nature as nature but as a piece of visual culture which, since the seventeenth century, has been influenced by the eye's technical armaments and subject to their

historical developments. Even convinced nature ontologists who claim that nature exists outside human culture are compelled to modify their standpoint in view of the power of technological visual media. By analogy with Walter Benjamin's theory about the loss of aura in art, the philosopher Gernot Böhme ponders the whereabouts of nature in the age of technical reproducibility. He comes to the conclusion that, through this reproducibility, nature loses "… what nature is, its definition through its opposite, through technology, culture, civilisation, the human sphere. This means that nature … itself must be understood as a cultural product, as 'socially constituted nature.'"[6] Nevertheless, against the background of the environmental issue, Böhme also regards the reverse to be true: "… that man, with all of his culture and technical possibilities, increasingly thinks of himself as something belonging to nature."[7]

This is the very consideration underlying the video installation "The Theater of Memory" (ill. 4) by the American Bill Viola, also on view on the lower level. Viola's media installation leads us quite close to the centre responsible for the world's technological transformation—the human brain—where it then confronts us with a primeval natural object, namely a tree (plate pp. 128/129). A tree, complete with roots, has been torn out of the ground and the tips of its branches draped with a network of nervously flickering lanterns. On the wall a video image glimmers every bit as restlessly, vague pictures now and then emerging from its indistinct patterns. Loudspeakers drone with an unidentifiable noise interrupted by phases of total silence. In "The Theater of Memory" we undertake an inward journey to our own neural regions, where we encounter a tree in the place of millions and millions of nerve cells. An external natural object thus becomes a metaphor for the internal nature of our brain. The branches are the dendrites (nerve endings) from which the neural impulses (flickering lanterns) spring over to neighbouring cells. Brain physiologists have discovered that the glistening of these darting sparks forms a pattern reflecting the overall current form of our ideas and memories. And the dark voids between the nerve endings are what trigger the transmission of impulses. "All our thoughts have at their center this small point of nothingness," says Viola, describing his theatre of memory. As we subject our senses to this process in the installation, our consciousness suddenly short-circuits, for the noises and flashing images we hear and see in the darkened space correspond precisely to what we perceive physiologically. Cast into the darkness of our brain, we suddenly become spectators of our own cerebral theatre of memories. Viola has repeatedly linked the physiological processes of perception with the iconography of external images, in many cases the image of the tree.

In adherence to the idea that inward and outward nature emerge from a common source—a central aspect of Jungian theory—Viola's electronically alienated images evoke a sense of metaphysical depth. In marked contrast to Rodney Graham: Impressive as the monumental tree stumps of his cedar photographs are, Graham's photohistorical reflections oppose the "magic of technically produced pictures": Through a trick of reversal, the artist intervenes with an awareness of the medium.

We have become acquainted with two contrary tendencies in the artistic treatment of the phenomenon of the tree and of nature: as embodied by artists like Long, Laib and Penone who conceive of their art as a renewal of proximity to nature, and by artists like Graham and Viola, who focus on the loss of nature in the age of technical reproduction and on nature's comprehensive destruction. What the two standpoints have in common is the realisation that the tree as an intact unit is gradually disappearing from sight. I alluded above to the idea that, through the dispersion and fragmentation of our life structures, the tree is losing relevance as an image of wholeness and oneness. In the history of civilisation, the tree has not only been presented as a natural phenomenon but also, repeatedly, as a metaphor for societal interrelationships. Piet Mondrian, for example, based his universal pictorial structure of a future society of balance on the image of branchwork. We might carry this thought further by asking what role the "image of the tree" could play in the future society of communication.

The answer may well be: the role of a counter-image, for in the past few decades civilisational developments have tended to be compared to other, aesthetically less appealing growths. In the 1970s, against the background of growing pluralism and increasingly difficult-to-control mechanic concatenations, the French philosophers Deleuze and Guattari popularised the image of the rampantly growing rhizome—quite a contrast to the hieratically organised shape of the rhizophoric tree. Today the term network is often used in connection with the breakneck development of communication technology—an image comparable to the unshapely mycelium of fungi. What is more, disruptions within this networked universe are caused by subversive data units quite similar in function to viruses. And finally, developments on the financial markets increasingly resemble the biological image of tumours.

III. 5
Bill Viola,
The Theater of Memory,
1985

These metaphors may not be pleasing to the imagination; nevertheless the comparison serves to isolate the context within which the aesthetic phenomenon of the tree must concentrate its power of expression. The upright shape of the tree can henceforth serve only as a counter-image, the symbol of a proud and protection-meriting remnant of nature.

1   Konrad Paul Liessmann: "Natura Mortua - Über das Verhältnis von Ästhetik und Ökologie" in *Kunstforum International,*
    Vol. 93, Cologne 1988, p. 71.

2   Cf. Donald Kuspit: "Wolfgang Laibs mystische Revolution" in *Wolfgang Laib* (exhibition catalogue), Kunstmuseum Bonn,
    1992, pp. 13-17.

3   Cf. Gérard Raulet: *Natur und Ornament,* Darmstadt 1987, pp. 117ff.

4   Liessmann, p. 71 and: "To employ art as a rescuer, as suggested by artists who subscribe to the ecology movement,
    would be foolish. Flirting with the pastoral and the idyllic is not the rescue of nature but the corruption of art through the
    clichés of tourist-branch advertising." p. 70.

5   The term was coined by Marlies Grütherich in the 1960s to refer to artists of the so-called Arte Povera movement:
    Mario Merz, Giovanni Anselmo, Penone himself and others.

6   Gernot Böhme: *Natürlich Natur,* Frankfurt a.M., 1992, p. 123.

7   Ibid.

89 GIUSEPPE PENONE · TREE ELEVEN METRES LONG · 1975 · 440^1/$_2$ x 10", Diameter 4^3/$_4$"

74 RICHARD LONG · PUGET SOUND DRIFTWOOD CIRCLE · 1996 · Diameter 276"

KY SKY SKY SKY SKY SKY SKY SKY SKY SKY SKY SKY

KY SKY SKY SKY SKY SKY SKY SKY SKY CLOUD SKY SKY

CLOUD CLOUD SKY SKY SKY SKY CLOUD CLOUD CLOUD

REE SKY SKY SKY SKY SKY SKY SKY SKY CLOUD SKY SKY

REE TREE SKY RAVEN SKY SKY SKY SKY SKY SKY SKY

WALKING JOURNEY SKY SKY SKY SKY SKY SKY SKY SKY

PATHS TREE TREE SKY SKY SKY SKY SKY SKY SKY SKY

T DAY OF MAY TREE SKY SKY SKY SKY SKY RAVEN SKY SKY

NO RIVER IN WAKAYAMA TREE TREE SKY SKY SKY SKY

HE MIYA RIVER IN ISE TREE TREE TREE SKY SKY SKY SKY

MISAKI KUMANOHONGU TREE TREE TREE SKY SKY SKY

MOUNT HIEI MIUNE YAMA TREE TREE TREE SKY SKY

APAN 1996 TREE TREE TREE TREE TREE TREE TREE SKY

SEA SEA SEA SEA SEA SEA SEA SEA SEA SEA SEA SEA SEA

53 **RODNEY GRAHAM** · STANLEY PARK CEDAR, VANCOUVER · 1991 · 106^1/$_2$ x 73^1/$_2$"

100 BILL VIOLA · THE THEATER OF MEMORY · 1985 · 158 x 188 x 330"

Christian Kaufmann

The Magic of Trees—Powers in Wood

Images from South Pacific Cultures

To many people still living under the spell of old cultural traditions in the rainforest and savannah areas of the tropical belt, trees are creatures like animals or humans. As a matter of fact, upon closer inspection, ethnological reports reveal that humans are often regarded as alternative manifestations of trees. According to this vision, trees were sometimes inverted to stand not on their heads but on their legs: The thick end of the trunk rises up, topped by the growth and control centre—in humans the head—above which the roots (hair) reach skyward. Below the head is the central trunk—the body with its vital organs—furnished with long branches or extremities.

The image of the inverted tree is connected with a number of very different levels of meaning. In the South Pacific, for instance, depending upon the conception of the world which evolved in each particular region or place, one finds the vision of the world tree as well as that of the evolution of primal forms of life into specifically human ones. The Pacific islanders' world tree originally stands upright, has deep roots and—as suggested by the branches of giant trees of the primeval forest—various platforms; its trunk and the lianas sprouting upward from it thus connect the earthly and heavenly spheres. In primitive times the moon woman is often quite explicitly bound to the tree, as with the aid of a liana. The link between the primeval and human worlds is formed by divine beings responsible for the decisive transformation from primitive times to the present, from the mythical otherworld to here-and-now reality. These beings often appear to humans as heroic figures, seen simultaneously as demigods—by virtue of which they are immortal—and semihuman ancestors who, emerging from the divine primeval world, brought man the knowledge and institutions essential for human life. Among these heroic mediators are those whose divine appearance is that of a tree prevalent in the respective region. Not surprisingly, images of those particular ancestral figures were carved from the wood of that tree. Examples on view in the exhibition are the figure of the Urungenam-like ancestral creator from the Biwat region on the Yuat River in Northern New Guinea, the supporting post of a men's ceremonial house of Kingaui on the central Sepik River (New Guinea)—decorated with the waves of the mythical primordial water—and the standing slit gong from the island of Ambrym in Vanuatu (ill. 1).

Various evidence found in Melanesia supports the assumption that hardwood was regarded as a manifestation of the relationship with the bony or "hard" ancestral substance passed along primarily through the paternal line of descent. In its many forms, the culturally influenced expression of this image suggests power and vitality—as in the form of stake-like tuberous plants, more specifically the long yam with which the figure of Urungenam is directly associated in the myth—as well as inertness and duration. A sculpture of the cultural hero thus refers to much more than a mere tree trunk (plate p. 137).

The use of elements which correspond to visions revolving around the durability of dense, hard woods was an obvious choice for the construction and furnishings of ceremonial houses. To some extent these structures were conceived as embodiments of primeval ancestors, for example in the crocodile shape of the Sepik region or on the Gulf of Papua in New Guinea. The image of these beings is quite strongly influenced by the vision of a "skin," consisting mate-

Ill. 1
Standing slit gong.
On the islands surrounding Malakula in Central Vanuatu, Melanesia, large standing slit gongs signify the presence of the common ancestors' bodies and voices. They stand in the core section of the ceremonial/dancing grounds, the special form of each individual gong representing the rank and privileges of its patron.

rially of the building's roof, facades and walls. The skin, the outer appearance, conceals the hard inner core—a distinction commonly made in Melanesia. The outer skin itself can be extremely resistant, like the skin of a full-grown crocodile.

In the ancestral context, the crocodile is also imagined as a transport vessel for human beings. The dugout canoes (without outriggers) of the Sepik region allude to this idea in a variety of different forms (ill. 2). In other regions of Oceania as well, the hull carved of a single tree symbolises a group of closely related persons. Water and the "skin" of the tree thus become complementary elements of the conception of the world.

III. 2
Supporting post of a men's ceremonial house.
The posts in the men's ceremonial houses of Iatmul in the Sepik area of Papua New Guinea lend the imagined events of creation a concrete appearance. Each men's house contains a platform, raised above the ground, its supports serving as references to the founders of the clans residing there. The concept of time is not based on the image of an axis of infinite length, but rather on the convergence of primeval times and the present in spatial coexistence. Accordingly, the portraits of several ancestors in the Wolimbit men's house of Kanganaman step directly from the tree-trunk supports into the present.

A further important form of mythical-artistic skin with an implicit relationship to water is seen in the so-called tapa, South Pacific bast cloth pounded from tree bark (plate pp. 148/149). The packing of masks in this material can have a spectacular effect—as exhibited by the speaking-pipe mask of Baining (New Britain) in the entry hall, a piece belonging to the Fondation Beyeler. While in reality it is the supporting structure of bamboo and liana which is wrapped, symbolically it is the mask bearer himself, through whose movements and actions the mask takes effect. Whereas to the European beholder the bark cloth appears as a textile, those who give or receive tapa as an object of exchange are quite aware of its origins in tree bark. Giving this material to someone often serves to designate the recipient as a bearer of spiritual-religious powers and to create a connection—by laying out the tapa to mark a pathway—as well as a protective distance between the person and his environment: Tapa keeps spiritual powers from developing damaging effects.

The bast usually comes from the paper mulberry tree (*Broussonetia papyrifera*); other suitable sources are the breadfruit tree and the rubber plant. Tapa is made by pounding the bast fibres of the bark—kept damp with water throughout the long process—into a supple cloth. In Polynesia, Micronesia and Melanesia, this task appears to have been carried out primarily by women. The pieces of cloth, which can measure as much as 2 x 4 metres, are glued together to obtain dimensions of up to 50 metres in length and 2 to 8 metres in width.

These expanses of cloth are often richly painted or otherwise patterned. In this form *tapa* serves primarily as a ceremonial offering and measure of wealth. Yet in a positive sense it also binds spiritual powers, particularly in creating connections between the living and the dead. Whereas on the one hand corpses are shrouded in lengths of tree bark cloth, *tapa* strips are also used among the living to symbolise the memory of and connection with the dead. On Rarotonga and elsewhere in Polynesia, the holy and powerful wooden sculptures of sacred figures were rolled in *tapa* to protect those charged with tending them. A particularly sensational use of *tapa* was the shrouding of chiefs and highly ranking women in several layers of cloth, again quite comparable to a packing process. The most fascinating performance of this act takes place when—as in the presentation of *tapa* to a new chief on Fiji—the heavy, pleated vestment is removed from its wearer with a single turn of the hand and falls down, revealing the person—the bringer of the offering—in his human nakedness. Following the ceremonies, particularly in Western Polynesia but also at mask festivals of the Baining (New Britain), the painted lengths of trunk bast cloth are often cut to pieces. The work thus lives on only in memory or, at best, in material fragments.

Let us return to the ceremonial houses. In many places these buildings—much like outdoor ceremonial sites surrounded by sacred trees—have the function of using spatial/artistic means to present the world—a thing created by divine forces—as something finite, in a certain sense to make it directly perceptible (ill. 3). In this respect they are comparable to the cathedrals of the Middle Ages. In mythical images of the world, the sphere of the divine beings and primeval forces is often located in the direct vicinity of the human sphere, although clear demarcations keep the two distinctly separate. The bearers of creative powers are conceivably capable at any instant of unpredictably stepping from the primeval otherworld into the human here and now.

An Abelam myth, for example, describes the way in which a mighty ancestral creator can change his form from that of the ceremonial house ridgepole to that of the primordial pig. According to investigations by Brigitta Hauser-Schäublin, the diagonal ridgepole represents the path of the rising sun, connecting the earthly East with the heavenly zenith. The story also relates how the ridgepole ancestor occasionally leaves his place in the shape of a man and intervenes in the human world as a kidnapper. The humans take revenge by attempting to drive him away with fire. Thus, in addition to ceremonial houses or sites–central places and axes–trees are the most important mediators between the worlds of the primeval past and the present, followed by animated stones, water and certain animals.

III. 3
Dugout canoe.
In the amphibious landscapes of the tropics, man and dugout canoe are inseparable companions. Faces from the sphere of the superhuman creators–which in the area of the Lower Sepik and its outlet (in the north of the island of New Guinea) appear chiefly in the shape of crocodile and birds' heads–aid human beings in finding their way and resisting threats.

In Melanesia, however, the idea of the superhuman powers harboured by trees and taking effect through them is by no means limited to the one aspect linking hardwood and bones as images of the ancestral substance. Other widely known myths tell for example of the emergence of fire. In these accounts the bearer of the original fire is a woman in the shape of a tree. Deep within itself, the tree conceals fire, a phenomenon which can actually occur in very old giant trees with rotting heartwood and still-living sapwood. Usually a demigod finds the fire quite unsuspectingly in the vagina of the mythical woman. It should be pointed out that in most of the religions of Melanesia as well as tropical Africa, divine power–both as imagined in ceremonial rites and magical acts as actually experienced–is referred to and perceived as "hot." Fire is the primary source of this power, and it comes from the wood of certain trees. Before the invention of matches and more modern lighters, the generation and maintenance of fire were tasks of central significance because of their life-preserving necessity as well as their mental and emotional proximity to the religious power of "heat." The old kindling tools of the rainforest cultures always consisted of a passive part, designated as feminine or quite directly as a "vagina," and a masculine part, often referred to as a "penis." Thus magical powers were thought to be inherent in the trees and plants whose technical attributes made them suitable for the production of fire ploughs–the most prevalent type of friction kindler. What is more, these powers were basically considered to be characteristic of all wood, as perceived most clearly in slowly burning, hotly glowing logs. It is above all the power of glowing embers which, for example in the Sepik region of New Guinea, is transmitted to clay pots during the firing process; it is also conveyed via the breath of the yam planter to his seedlings to promote their growth in the greatest numbers and most impressive form possible.

European readers with an Occidental understanding of culture might be wondering why I have not yet referred to the vegetative power of wood, particularly the mysteries of a young tree in sap. For one thing, most tropical plants do not undergo the seasonal changes of withering in the autumn and sprouting, shooting and flowing with sap in the spring. Even the growth fluctuations caused by alternations between a drier season and a damper and hotter season are usually not extreme enough to cause the formation of regular growth rings in trees.

Furthermore, the image of sprouting and the power of fast growth is quite often associated with bamboo and other reed plants as well as woody plants suitable for use as arrow bows, whereas the maternal-vegetative power is expressly ascribed to palms. And palms are in many ways quite different from trees.

The first of these two powers finds expression in the legends of the Marind-anim (Southwestern New Guinea), in which the strung bow (made of bamboo or palm bark) embodies a male dema or cultural hero from his "nose" to his "foot" (ill. 4). He is caught in the embrace of his wife, the bamboo string, and accompanied by their daughters. Humans must combine their efforts to kill the couple in order to replace their older hunting weapons—simple clubs—with more effective ones. In the heat of the battle, however, the Marind-anim and their neighbours become divided when one group succeeds in acquiring the arrowheads made of cassowary bones and kangaroo claws and the other the empty arrow shafts of reed.

III. 4
Figure of a the *Bow Dema,* Marind-anim, Southwestern New Guinea, Irian Java. Demas are cultural heroes who transmitted important elements of nature (e.g. the banana or sago palm and game animals as sustenance) and culture (e.g. the act of hunting and the bow as a weapon) to man. The original dema is still concealed in the simple Marind-anim bow, its "nose"—i.e. face—appearing at the top, its "foot " at the bottom.

In the botanical sense, due to their clustered, hose-like venation structure, palms can be classified neither as reeds, bushes nor trees. Only their outer bark becomes woody, providing material for the most resistant spears. In tropical cultures, palms are also often classified differently from trees in the ideational context.

Certain coconut palms form a woody trunk, but this wood is only used in places—such as the small, densely populated atolls—which lack the required amount of suitable tree wood. On the other hand, the hardness and eyes of the coconut shell lead to an analogy with the human skull, a powerful image quite prevalent even today in the idiomatic speech of Melanesia.

Due to its great usefulness, the palm tree—i.e. the coconut, the sago, the sugar and the areca or betel palm as well as certain types of climbing palms and the palm-like pandanus—plays as outstanding a role in these peoples' economic lives as it does in their mythology. Although no bamboo or palm sculptures could be included in the exhibition, they do exist, as proven by the dema figures of the above-mentioned Marind-anim (Southwestern New Guinea) on view in the Museum der Kulturen in Basle. As a matter of fact, these figures are apt illustrations of the complexity of world conceptions developed by extremely old cultures, particularly with regard to their treatment of nature. In a remarkable way, these ancient peoples linked their images of the powers of nature, i.e. the powers dominating their own environments, with forces originating in the acts of certain gods or even other human beings. Nature is not regarded by man simply as an animated other-entity, as assumed by the theory of animism. On the contrary, it is an absolutely essential link between human beings and their divine ancestors, a living and irreplaceable part of both worlds simultaneously.

To reduce things to a common denominator, the same spiritual powers of divine origin animate both man and his environment: There is no fundamental man-nature dichotomy, nor can there be any basic spatial or temporal separation of the divine from the human. From every level of the world, influence is exerted on every other level along certain spatial paths and temporal axes which evolve cyclically, not linearly and one-dimensionally. Wood plays an important role as a medium for the transmission of effects and effectiveness. A further aspect also demands consideration here: the fact that, before the introduction of metal tools, the carver and shaper of wood had to feel his way into his material much more intensively: not only "tame" it with his physical powers but also approach it spiritually, to the point of intimacy. Successful works thus radiated an especially impressive force, pulsating just beneath their intricately worked surfaces: The chip-removing cut of the stone blade in the adze was shorter and often narrower than that of the plane iron which later replaced it. Other decisive changes occurred when the old notching, scratching, scraping and drilling devices—made of rodent teeth, hog tusks, seashells and snail shells as well as fragments of obsidian and flint—were supplanted by metal knives. Even the treatment of the surface with natural "files"—made of rough leaves, sand and ray skin—instead of metal ones, and the rubbing of the carved surfaces with fine clay sediment or the saps, resins and oils of plants contribute to the impression of a form fashioned with the utmost dedication down the last detail.

Striking examples of the outstanding role played by wood as a workable material were produced by the Asmat. According to their imagery, the first humans were fashioned from wood by a divine carver and brought to life with the sound of a tubular drum made of a hollowed tree trunk. A group of works in the Museum der Kulturen in Basle illustrates this act of creation. In this culture, headhunting serves not to destroy but to renew vital energy.

A very similar Oceanian story of creation is associated with the *yipwon*, figures of hunting aides from the area of the Korewori River in the Sepik region (plate p. 138). These figures serve as temporary residents for spirits which come to the hunter's as well as the warrior's aid. In addition, they function as cult instruments in the men's ceremonial house, where the respective spirits are invoked and brought offerings. The yipwon actually came into existence involuntarily when, at the end of a long search, the Sun Man finally found a tree suitable for the making of a slit gong: His mother's—the moon woman's—older sister had transformed herself into a tree by sticking her head into the earth. Children of the Sun Man, the *yipwon*, emerged from the chips cut away during the carving of the wood. Then, however, they assaulted and killed a kinsman of the Sun and drank his blood. In a state of fright, caused by their discovery that the moon had witnessed their crime, the yipwon stretched themselves out broad and thin on the wall of the men's ceremonial house. In fulfilment of his divine mission, Sun Man then rose to heaven, leaving man behind and bestowing upon him the hunting animals and rituals as well as the *yipwon* figures to aid him during the hunt.

Bibliography

Catalogue of the Fondation Beyeler Collection. Prestel, Munich and New York, 1997

Haberland, Eike, *The Caves of Karawari.* D'Arcy Galleries, New York, 1968

Haberland, Eike and Siegfried Seyfarth, *Die Yimar am oberen Korewori.* Studien zur Kulturkunde Vol. 36. Wiesbaden, 1974

Hauser-Schäublin, Brigitta, *Kulthäuser in Nord-Neuguinea.* Abhandlungen und Berichte des Staatlichen Museums für Völkerkunde Dresden, Vol. 43. Berlin, 1989

Kaeppler, Adrienne, Christian Kaufmann and Douglas Newton, *Oceanic Art.* Abrams, New York, 1998

Kaufmann, Christian, "Ozeanien" in: *Catalogue of the Fondation Beyeler Collection.* Prestel, Munich and New York, 1997

Münzl, Mark (Ed.), *Neuguinea – Nutzung und Deutung der Umwelt,* Series Roter Faden durch das Museum für Völkerkunde Frankfurt am Main, 2 Vols., 1987

Wirz, Paul, *Die Marind-anim von Holländisch-Süd-Neu-Guinea,* Abhandlungen aus dem Gebiet der Auslandskunde, Vols. 10 and 16, Hamburg, Friederichsen, 1922 and 1925

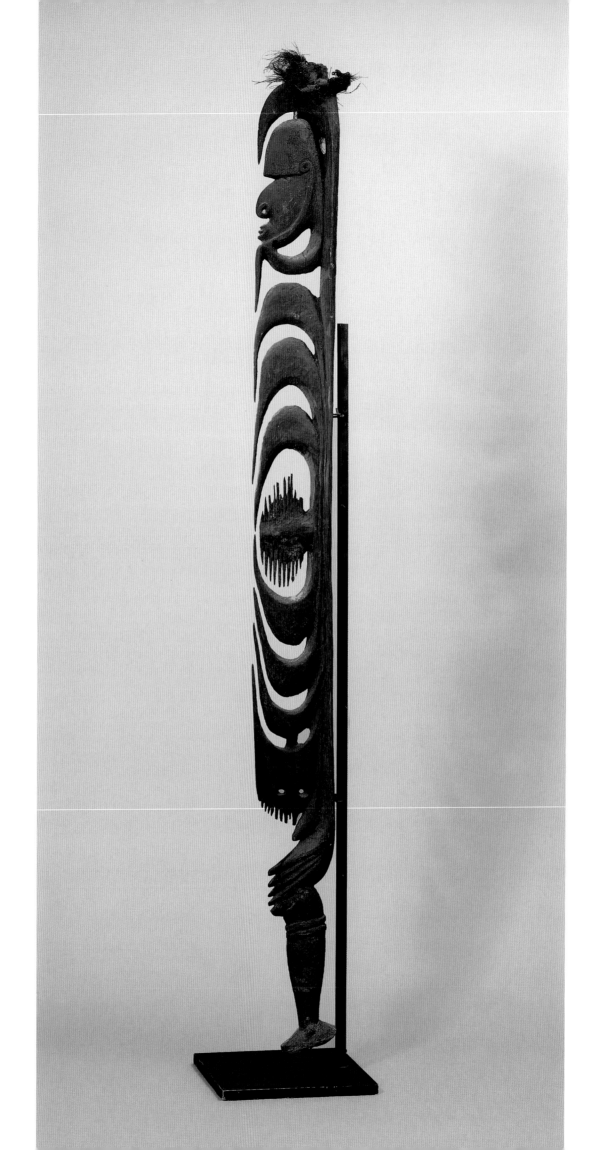

103 ANCESTRAL FIGURE, EASTERN IATMUL OR SOUTHERN NEIGHBOURS · Height 53¹/₂"

111   DANCING PADDLE, RAPA · Height 30"

109 MASK, KEPONG OR MATUA · Height 30"

106   MALE FIGURE, NALIK · 19ᵀᴴ CENTURY · Height 55"

107 MALE FIGURE, NALIK · 18TH/19TH CENTURY · Height 71¹/₂"

Bernhard Gardi

Trees—Powers in Wood
Conceptions of African Art

Forest, primeval mother! The various pygmy groups of the equatorial rain forest perceive their so richly vegetated environment as feminine. Men and women on nutrition-seeking trips communicate with one another by means of loud yodelling. On the ground, far below the treetops, a human being feels lost, alone and vulnerable. The yodel, cutting through the nearly absolute silence of the forest, helps him to set a boundary between himself and nature, and to ward off his fear.

Some 4,000 different species of trees are native to northwestern Gabon. For many centuries, this seemingly impenetrable forest was the scene of migrations brought about by the influx of the Fang and giving rise to one of the most splendid art styles of Africa. To aid them in the process of assimilation to the new environment, the immigrants brought their ancestors with them: portable bark cases containing the skulls, bones, or jewellery of the deceased and "decorated" with a head or figure affixed to the top. The oil extracted from the fruits of the oil palm was sacrificed to these "guard figures" or *biery*.

The great *nkisi n'konde* also stems from the equatorial rain forest, more specifically from the old Kingdom of Congo (ill. 1). The first Portuguese reports of this kingdom on the mouth of the Zaire River date back to before the discovery of America. Human actions were ruled by powers created and predetermined by God, so-called *minkisi* (plural of *nkisi*), which occur everywhere in nature—not least of all in trees—and can have both a harmful as well as a healing effect. Specialists (or "men of knowledge," "priests") learned to master these powers during an apprenticeship lasting many years. Certain carved figures which the specialist could buy at the market were also called *minkisi*. Such a figure had no power,

Congo   Fétiches du Ka-Kongo

Nels, Bruxelles Série 14 No. 131

III. 1
Three different *minkisi* (plural of *nkisi*). Setting arranged for photograph. Postcard

however, until it had been "magically charged" by a "man of knowledge": The opening carved into the middle of its body for this purpose was filled with a resinous compound in which a great variety of ingredients—soil, bark, crystal, the teeth of rodents—were imbedded. The opening was then sealed by a cowry shell or a small European mirror (plate p. 155).

Whereas the reliquary figure of the Fang was intended for ritual use within a particular lineage, the large *nkisi* figure—an aid in the regulation of everyday village life—belonged to a specialist and earned him income. The carefully executed ears and eyes, complete with eyebrows, as well as the mouth, opened to reveal a tongue, are references to the ability of such a figure to listen, see and speak. Through the mediation of a specialist, communication with other powers was possible. Every fragment of iron pounded into the figure indicated that a consultation had taken place with the specialist and contact with the spirits successfully made. In the case of both figure types, however, the artwork so greatly appreciated by us Europeans was subordinate in importance to the inherent idea, manifested in a *biery* by the preserved relics of the ancestors, in a *nkisi n'konde* by the additive elements symbolising this people's conception of the world.

Mumuye. We are in the open land, in the wide landscape south of the Benue River. Hills, rocks and stony ground characterise the scenery. The houses are no longer rectangular, as in the rain forest, but round. In former times there were no real villages here; the land was speckled with individual farmsteads nestling against the terraced slopes of mountains.

The people planted euphorbia bushes to mark special sites regarded as sacred and harbouring figures which only the masters of the earth were allowed to consult. Practically nothing is known about the significance of these highly abstract and different-sized sculptures, of which the one in the Fondation Beyeler is surely the most expressive and beautiful (plate p. 152). Apparently, however, they were used to carry out a variety of functions such as divination, healing or rainmaking.

The Senufo of the northern Ivory Coast live on much more fertile land. Their sometimes quite large villages are divided into quarters, each possessing a "bois sacré," a "sacred grove" which foreigners are strictly prohibited from entering. In former times, important masks, statues and music instruments were stored in inconspicuous huts in the midst of these small forests, and cult objects are kept there even today. For the Senufo, the legendary secret society *poro* is by no means extinct. Travellers to this region are particularly struck by the mightiness of the trees and the impermeable underbrush of the sacred groves (ill. 2). A piece of virgin forest in the savannah! One can begin to imagine what the vegetation here would look like if not for the intervention of man.

A particularly mighty savannah tree, towering over every grove, is the fromager. Its thick trunk and huge crown are supported by widely outstretched roots. Many an explorer laden with crates of bartering objects found an easily defensible spot in the niches formed by the supraterranean rootwork of this tree. Officers of the region's first military stations likewise recognised the advantages offered by the thickness of the giant trunks, sometimes turning them into watchtowers (ill. 3).

Bibliography

Till Förster, *Die Kunst der Senufo,* exhibition catalogue, Museum Rietberg, Zurich, 1988

Bernhard Gardi, *Zaïre. Masken, Figuren,* exhibition catalogue, Museum für Völkerkunde Basel, Basle, 1986

Annette Hladik, "Structure et production de la forêt dense," in: *Se nourrir en forêt équatoriale,* UNESCO, Claude Marcel Hladik, Serge Bahuchet, Igor de Garine, eds., Paris, 1989

Arnold Rubin, "Mumuye, Figs. 91, 92," in: *For Spirits and Kings. African Art from the Tishman Collection,* Susan Vogel, ed., exhibition catalogue, The Metropolitan Museum of Art, New York, 1981

Robert Farris Thompson, "Naissance du dessin 'nègre': L'art mbuti dans une perspective mondiale," in: *Pygmées? Peintures sur écorce battue des Mbuti (Haut-Zaïre),* exhibition catalogue, Musée Dapper, Paris, 1991

117 POUNDING FIGURE, DEBLE · ca. 1870 · Height 37¹/₂"
120 CULT FIGURE · 19ᵀᴴ OR EARLY 20ᵀᴴ CENTURY · Height 39"

118 FEMALE RELIQUARY FIGURE, BIERY · 19TH/20TH CENTURY · Height 17¹/₂"

121   NAIL FIGURE, NKISI N'KONDE · before 1900 · Height 41"

119 MALE ANCESTRAL FIGURE, LUSINGITI · 19ᵀᴴ/20ᵀᴴ CENTURY · Height 36¹/₂"

122   SITTING FIGURE · PRESUMABLY 17ᵀᴴ/18ᵀᴴ CENTURY · Height 32", depth 21"

Works on Exhibit

Cuno Amiet
Solothurn 1868 – 1961 Oschwand

1
Winter Landscape, 1904
Winterlandschaft
Oil on asbestos cement, $21^{1}/_{2}$ x $25^{1}/_{2}$"
Kunstmuseum Solothurn
Plate p. 68

2
Apple Harvest, 1907
Apfelernte
Oil on canvas, 40 x $40^{1}/_{4}$"
Kunstmuseum Solothurn
Plate p. 67

3
Winter, 1958
Winter
Oil and tempera on canvas, $39^{1}/_{4}$ x $36^{1}/_{2}$"
Kunstmuseum Bern
Plate p. 69

Hans Arp
Strasbourg 1886 – 1966 Basle

4
Shell Tree, 1960
Schalenbaum
Bronze, No. 0/3, $78^{1}/_{2}$ x $39^{1}/_{2}$ x $42^{1}/_{4}$"
Stiftung Hans Arp und Sophie Taeuber-Arp e.V.
Plate p. 101

Georg Baselitz
Deutschbaselitz (Saxony) 1938

5
The Tree, 1966
Der Baum
Oil on canvas, $64^{3}/_{4}$ x 52"
Sammlung Froehlich, Stuttgart
Plate p. 104

6
Birch Trees, 1973
Birken
Ink on paper, $15^{1}/_{4}$ x $12^{1}/_{4}$"
Öffentliche Kunstsammlung Basel,
Kupferstichkabinett

7
Birch Trees, 1973
Birken
Ink and India ink on paper, $15^{1}/_{4}$ x $12^{1}/_{4}$"
Öffentliche Kunstsammlung Basel,
Kupferstichkabinett

8
Shrubbery, 1975
Gebüsch
Oil on canvas, 80 x $64^{3}/_{4}$"
Collection T, Switzerland
Plate p. 105

9
Mother of the Garland, 13. XI. 96
Mutter der Girlande
Charcoal and blue oil paint on limewood,
$12^{1}/_{2}$ x $37^{1}/_{2}$ x $32^{1}/_{2}$"
Kunstmuseum Bonn, Permanent loan from
Sammlung Hans Grothe
Plate p. 106

Max Beckmann
Leipzig 1884 – 1950 New York

10
West Park, 1950
West-Park
Oil on canvas, $55^{3}/_{4}$ x $24^{1}/_{2}$"
Private collection
Plate p. 79

Pierre Bonnard
Fontenay-aux-Roses 1867 – 1947 Le Cannet
(near Cannes)

11
The Almond Tree in Bloom, 1946/47
L'Amandier en fleurs
Oil on canvas, 22 x 15"
Musée national d'art moderne / Centre de création industrielle, Centre Georges Pompidou, Paris
Plate p. 75

Georges Braque
Argenteuil 1882 – 1963 Paris

12
Landscape at l'Estaque, 1906
Paysage à l'Estaque
Oil on canvas, $50^{1}/_{2}$ x $24^{1}/_{2}$"
Private collection
Plate p. 38

Samuel Buri
Täuffelen (on the Bieler See) 1935

13
Apple Power, 1979
Oil on canvas, $81^{1}/_{4}$ x $81^{1}/_{4}$"
In private ownership
Plate p. 109

Alexander Calder
Philadelphia 1898 – 1976 New York

14
Leaves and Tripod, ca. 1939
Sheet metal, metal rods, wire, $94^{1}/_{2}$ x 66"
Galerie Beyeler, Basle
Plate p. 102

15
The Tree, 1966
Steel, painted, 208 x 428"
Fondation Beyeler, Riehen/Basle
Plate p. 103

Paul Cézanne
Aix-en-Provence 1839 – 1906 Aix-en-Provence

16
The Bridge of Maincy, 1879/80
Le Pont de Maincy
Oil on canvas, 24 x $29^{1}/_{4}$"
Musée d'Orsay, Paris; Acquired with funds from an anonymous Canadian donation, 1955
Plate p. 31

17
Boulders, Pine Trees and Sea at l'Estaque,
1883–1885
L'Estaque – Rochers, Pins et Mer
Oil on canvas, 40 x $32^{1}/_{2}$"
Staatliche Kunsthalle Karlsruhe
Plate p. 33

18
Trees, ca. 1887
Arbres
Pencil on paper, $8^{1}/_{2}$ x $5^{1}/_{4}$"
Öffentliche Kunstsammlung Basel,
Kupferstichkabinett

116 HEADDRESS, A MANTSHO-NA-TSHOL · 19TH/20TH CENTURY · Height 80" (plate p. 158)

19
Landscape near Aix–The Plain of the Arc River,
1892–1895
Paysage des environs d'Aix – La Plaine de l'Arc
Oil on canvas, 33 x 26$^{1}/_{4}$"
Carnegie Museum of Art, Pittsburgh; Acquired
through the generosity of the Sarah Mellon Scaife
Family, 1966
Plate p. 32

20
Forest Scene (Path from Mas Jolie to Château Noir),
1900–1902
Sous-Bois (Chemin du Mas Jolie au Château Noir)
Oil on canvas, 31$^{1}/_{4}$ x 25$^{1}/_{2}$"
Fondation Beyeler, Riehen/Basle
Plate p. 35

21
Road with Trees on a Slope, ca. 1904
Route avec arbres sur une pente
Water-colour and pencil on paper, 18$^{3}/_{4}$ x 12$^{1}/_{4}$"
Fondation Beyeler, Riehen/Basle
Plate p. 34

Marc Chagall
Vitebsk 1887 – 1985 St-Paul-de-Vence

22
Village in Autumn, 1939–1945
Village d'automne
Oil on canvas, 32$^{1}/_{2}$ x 26"
Wadsworth Atheneum, Hartford, Connecticut;
Gift of Mr. and Mrs. Alfred Jaretzki, Jr., Endowed
by Mr. and Mrs. Charles Gill, 1952.438

Christo
Gabrovo (Bulgaria) 1935
Jeanne-Claude
Casablanca 1935

23
*Wrapped Trees, Fondation Beyeler, Berower Park,
Riehen/Basle*, 1997/98
Polyester (cloth), acrylic (rope), 162 wrapped
trees, height 10–83,3'
Christo and Jeanne-Claude, 1997/98
Plate pp. 171, 172/173

Lovis Corinth
Tapiau (near Königsberg) 1858 - 1925 Zandvoort

24
Walchensee Landscape – View of the Wetterstein,
1921
Walchenseelandschaft – Blick auf Wetterstein
Oil on canvas, 36$^{1}/_{4}$ x 48"
Saarland Museum Saarbrücken, Stiftung Saar-
ländischer Kulturbesitz
Plate p. 65

Camille Corot
Paris 1796 - 1875 Paris

25
The Italian Villa Behind Pines, undated
La Villa italienne derriére les pins
Oil on canvas, 61$^{3}/_{4}$ x 44$^{3}/_{4}$"
Öffentliche Kunstsammlung Basel, Kunstmuseum
Plate p. 23

Gustave Courbet
Ornans (Franche-Comté) 1819 - 1877
La Tour-de-Peilz (near Vevey)

26
The Gust of Wind, ca. 1855
Le Coup de vent
Oil on canvas, 57$^{1}/_{2}$ x 91$^{1}/_{4}$"
In private ownership

André Derain
Chatou (near Paris) 1880 - 1954 near Garches

27
Landscape at l'Estaque, 1907
Paysage à l'Estaque
Oil on canvas, 29 x 36$^{1}/_{2}$"
Private collection
Plate p. 39

Jean Dubuffet
Le Havre 1901 - 1985 Paris

28
The Group of Trees, May 9, 1969
Le Boqueteau
Epoxy, painted with polyurethane,
38 x 55$^{1}/_{2}$ x 50$^{3}/_{4}$"
Fondation Dubuffet, Paris
Plate p. 99

Max Ernst
Brühl (near Cologne) 1891 - 1976 Paris

29
The Large Forest, 1927
La grande Forêt
Oil on canvas, 45$^{3}/_{4}$ x 58$^{1}/_{2}$"
Öffentliche Kunstsammlung Basel, Kunstmuseum
Plate p. 88

30
The Fascination of the Cypress, 1939
Le fascinant Cyprès
Oil on canvas, 29$^{1}/_{2}$ x 40"
Private collection
Plate p. 89

Caspar David Friedrich
Greifswald 1774 - 1840 Dresden

31
Oak Tree in the Snow, 1829
Eichbaum im Schnee
Oil on canvas, 28$^{1}/_{2}$ x 19$^{1}/_{4}$"
Staatliche Museen zu Berlin, Nationalgalerie
Frontispiece p. 6

Hamish Fulton
London 1946

32
Untitled, Japan 1996
Walltext
Vinyl letters, 171 x 356"
Collection Hamish Fulton
Plate p. 124/125

Alberto Giacometti
Borgonovo (near Stampa) 1901 - 1966 Chur

33
Figure Beneath a Tree, 1949
Figure sous un arbre
Coloured pencil on paper, coloured pencil study
on verso, 14 x 10$^{1}/_{4}$"
Succession Gérald Cramer, Geneva

34
The Glade, 1950
La Clairière
Bronze, 22$^{1}/_{2}$ x 23$^{1}/_{2}$ x 19$^{1}/_{2}$"
Fondation Marguerite et Aimé Maeght, Saint-Paul
Plate p. 93

35
The Forest, 1950
La Forêt
Bronze, No. 5/6, 23$^{1}/_{2}$ x 25$^{3}/_{4}$ x 24"
Wilhelm-Lehmbruck-Museum, Duisburg
Plate p. 95

36
Man in a Landscape, 1958
Homme dans un paysage
Oil on canvas, 24 x 32$^{1}/_{2}$"
Private collection, Switzerland
Plate p. 94

37
View from the Studio at Stampa, 1959
Vue de l'atelier à Stampa
Oil on canvas, 24 x 20"
Private collection, Switzerland
Plate p. 97

38
Large Standing Woman IV, 1960
Grande femme IV
Bronze, No. 3/6, height 106$^{1}/_{4}$"
Fondation Beyeler, Riehen/Basle

39
Tree, 1960
Arbre
Pencil on paper, 17³/₄ x 11¹/₂"
Öffentliche Kunstsammlung Basel,
Kupferstichkabinett

40
The Man and The Tree, 1962
L'Homme et l'arbre
Coloured pencil on paper, 14 x 10¹/₂"
Private collection, Switzerland

Vincent van Gogh
Groot-Zundert 1853 – 1890 Auvers-sur-Oise

41
Trees under Storm Clouds, 1885
Arbres sous un ciel d'orage
Black crayon, heightened with white,
on bluish-grey paper, 11¹/₂ x 9"
Van Gogh Museum Amsterdam
(Vincent van Gogh Foundation)

42
The Old Yew Tree, 1888
Le vieil If
Oil on canvas, 36³/₄ x 29"
Private collection
Plate p. 28

43
The Alyscamps, Avenue in Arles, 1888
Les Alyscamps, Avenue à Arles
Oil on canvas, 35¹/₂ x 28³/₄"
Private collection
Plate p. 27

44
The Sower, 1888
Le Semeur
Oil on jute on canvas, 29¹/₄ x 37"
Foundation E.G. Bührle Collection, Zurich
Plate p. 26

45
Tree Against the Wall of the Saint Paul Hospital,
1889
Arbres contre le mur de l'hôpital Saint Paul
Pencil, charcoal on thin paper, 12 x 8¹/₄"
Van Gogh Museum Amsterdam
(Vincent van Gogh Foundation)

46
Path Between Pine Trees, 1889
Sentier entre les pins
Black chalk, stumped on paper, 8 x 11¹/₂"
Van Gogh Museum Amsterdam
(Vincent van Gogh Foundation)

47
Pine Trees in the Garden of the Saint Paul Hospital,
1889
Pins dans le jardin de l'hôpital Saint Paul
Pencil and black chalk on thin paper,
10¹/₄ x 12³/₄"
Van Gogh Museum Amsterdam
(Vincent van Gogh Foundation)

48
Pine Trees Against an Evening Sky, 1889
Pins sur le ciel du soir
Oil on canvas, 36³/₄ x 29¹/₄"
Kröller-Müller Museum, Otterlo
Plate p. 29

Natalia Goncharova
Ladyschkino 1881 – 1962 Paris

49
Yellow and Green Forest, 1913
Oil on canvas, 41 x 34¹/₄"
Staatsgalerie Stuttgart
Plate p. 45

Rodney Graham
Vancouver 1949

50
Stanley Park Cedar, Vancouver, 1991
Colour print from black-and-white negative, No. 1,
106¹/₂ x 73¹/₂"
Galerie Nelson, Paris

51
Stanley Park Cedar, Vancouver, 1991
Colour print from black-and-white negative, No. 2,
106¹/₂ x 73¹/₂"
Collection du Musée départemental d'art
contemporain de Rochechouart

52
Stanley Park Cedar, Vancouver, 1991
Colour print from black-and-white negative, No. 3,
106¹/₂ x 73¹/₂"
Collection L. Declerck, Belgium

53
Stanley Park Cedar, Vancouver, 1991
Colour print from black-and-white negative, No. 6,
106¹/₂ x 73¹/₂"
Galerie Nelson, Paris
Plate p. 127

54
Stanley Park Cedar, Vancouver, 1991
Colour print from black-and-white negative, No. 8,
106¹/₂ x 73¹/₂"
Collection Anne-Marie et Marc Robelin

55
Lighthouse Park Cedar, Vancouver, 1991
Colour print from black-and-white negative,
106¹/₂ x 73¹/₂"
Courtesy Art & Public, Geneva

Ferdinand Hodler
Bern 1853 – 1918 Geneva

56
Apple Trees, 1897
Apfelbäume
Oil on canvas, 20³/₄ x 15¹/₂"
In private ownership
Plate p. 62

57
The Fir Tree (near Chamby), 1905
Die Tanne (bei Chambly)
Oil on canvas, 38¹/₂ x 26¹/₂"
In private ownership, Kilchberg Zurich
Plate p. 60

58
Cherry Tree in Bloom, 1905
Blühender Kirschbaum
Oil on canvas, 23¹/₂ x 18¹/₂"
Private collection
Plate p. 63

59
The Nut Tree, 1907
Der Nussbaum
Oil on canvas, 29 x 25¹/₂"
Private collection
Plate p. 62

60
Woodcutter, 1910
Holzfäller
Oil on canvas, 52 x 40¹/₂"
Private collection
Plate p. 61

Anselm Kiefer
Donaueschingen 1945

61
Tree with Palette, 1978
Baum mit Palette
Oil and lead on canvas, 110¹/₄ x 74³/₄"
Fondation Beyeler, Riehen/Basle
Plate p. 107

Ernst Ludwig Kirchner
Aschaffenburg 1880 – 1938 Frauenkirch
(near Davos)

62
Fehmarn Landscape – Forest Path, 1914
Fehmarnlandschaft – Waldweg
Oil on canvas, 48 x 36"
Private collection
Plate p. 76

63
Mountain Forest, 1918–1920
Bergwald
Oil on canvas, 32 x 28"
Kirchner Museum Davos; Donated by Franz and
Elsa Bruhin-Valtin, 1982
Plate p. 77

64
Sertig Path (Valley near Davos Frauenkirch), 1926
Sertigweg (Tal bei Davos Frauenkirch)
Pencil and water-colour on paper, 14^1/$_2$ x 18^1/$_4$"
Öffentliche Kunstsammlung Basel,
Kupferstichkabinett

Paul Klee
Münchenbuchsee (near Bern) 1879 – 1940
Muralto-Locarno

65
Abandoned Garden, 1909/55
verlassener Garten
Pen and black ink on paper, 12^3/$_4$ x 9^1/$_2$"
Öffentliche Kunstsammlung Basel,
Kupferstichkabinett

66
Landscape in Motion with Spherical Trees,
1920/124
Bewegte Landschaft mit Kugelbäumen
Oil on cartboard, 12^1/$_2$ x 37^1/$_2$"
Private collection, Switzerland
Plate p. 82

67
Forest Witches, 1938/145 (K5)
Waldhexen
Oil on paper on jute, 39^1/$_2$ x 29^1/$_2$"
Private collection
Plate p. 81

68
Deep in the Forest, 1939/554 (CC14)
tief im Wald
Mixed technique on canvas prepared
with oil ground, 20 x 17^1/$_4$"
Kunstsammlung Nordrhein-Westfalen, Düsseldorf
Plate p. 83

Gustav Klimt
Baumgarten (Vienna) 1862 – 1918 Vienna

69
The Large Poplar (II), also *"Rising Storm"*, 1903
Die grosse Pappel (II), auch "Aufsteigendes
Gewitter"
Oil on canvas, 40 x 40"
Leopold Museum – Private foundation, Vienna
Plate p. 56

70
Apple Tree II, ca. 1916
Apfelbaum II
Oil on canvas, 32 x 32"
Vienna, Österreichische Galerie Belvedere
Plate p. 57

Wolfgang Laib
Metzingen 1950

71
Pine Tree Pollen, 1998
Blütenstaub von Kiefern
Pine tree pollen (3 jars), ca. 88 x 104"
Wolfgang Laib; Courtesy Galerie
Konrad Fischer, Düsseldorf
Plate p. 123

Fernand Léger
Argentan 1881 – 1955 Gif-sur-Yvette

72
The Level Crossing, 1912
Le Passage à niveau
Oil on canvas, 37 x 32"
Fondation Beyeler, Riehen/Basle
Plate p. 43

Roy Lichtenstein
New York 1923 – 1997 New York

73
Painting in Landscape, 1984
Oil on canvas, 50 x 60"
Fondation Beyeler, Riehen/Basle
Plate p. 113

Richard Long
Bristol 1945

74
Puget Sound Driftwood Circle, 1996
Driftwood, diameter 276"
Courtesy Donald Young Gallery, Chicago
Plate p. 122

René Magritte
Lessines 1898 – 1967 Brussels

75
The Empire of Lights, 1948
L'Empire des lumières
Oil on canvas, 40 x 32"
Private collection, Switzerland
Plate p. 87

76
The Waterfall, 1961
La Cascade
Oil on canvas, 32^1/$_2$ x 40"
Private collection, Switzerland
Plate p. 86

Kasimir Malevich
Kiev 1878 – 1935 Leningrad

77
Landscape (Winter), 1909
Oil on canvas, 19^1/$_2$ x 21^1/$_2$"
Museum Ludwig, Cologne, Sammlung Ludwig
Plate p. 44

Henri Matisse
Le Cateau-Cambrésis 1869 – 1954 Cimiez
(near Nice)

78
The Pond at Trivaux, 1917
L'Étang de Trivaux
Oil on canvas, 36^1/$_2$ x 29^1/$_4$"
Tate Gallery, London; Bequeathed by C. Frank
Stoop, 1933; Formerly Collection Paul Guillaume
Plate p. 53

79
The Garden at Issy (The Studio in Clamart),
ca. 1917
Jardin à Issy (L'Atelier à Clamart)
Oil on canvas, 51 x 35"
Fondation Beyeler, Riehen/Basle
Plate p. 52

Piet Mondrian
Amersfoort 1872 – 1944 New York

80
Red Tree, 1908
Oil on canvas, 28 x 39^1/$_2$"
Collection Gemeentemuseum, The Hague, The
Netherlands
Plate p. 47

81
Eucalyptus Tree (Black), 1910
Oil on canvas, 20^1/$_2$ x 15^1/$_2$"
Private collection
Plate p. 48

82
Eucalyptus, 1912
Eucalyptus
Oil on canvas, 23³/₄ x 20¹/₂"
Fondation Beyeler, Riehen/Basle
Plate p. 49

83
Composition No. XVI (Composition I, Trees),
1912/13
Composition Nᵒ XVI (Composition I, Arbres)
Oil on canvas, 33¹/₂ x 29¹/₂"
Fondation Beyeler, Riehen/Basle
Plate p. 51

Claude Monet
Paris 1840 – 1926 Giverny

84
Poplars on the Banks of the Epte, Twilight, 1891
Peupliers au bord de l'Epte, crépuscule
Oil on canvas, 40 x 26"
Private collection, New York
Plate p. 24

85
Poplars on the Banks of the Epte, 1891
Peupliers au bord de l'Epte
Oil on canvas, 40 x 26"
Philadelphia Museum of Art; Bequest of Anne
Thomson in memory of her father Frank Thomson
and her mother Mary Elizabeth Clarke Thomson
Plate p. 25

86
Weeping Willow, 1920–1922
Saule pleurer
Oil on canvas, 44 x 40"
Private collection, Paris
Plate p. 74

Edvard Munch
Løten (Hedmark) 1863 – 1944 Hof Ekely near Oslo

87
Winter Night, 1900
Oil on canvas, 32¹/₄ x 48¹/₄"
Kunsthaus Zürich
Plate p. 55

88
The Red House in the Snow, 1925/26
Oil on canvas, 27¹/₄ x 36"
Staatsgalerie Stuttgart
Plate p. 54

Giuseppe Penone
Garessio 1947

89
Tree Eleven Metres Long, 1975
Albero di undici metri
Wood, 440¹/₂ x 10", diameter 4³/₄"
Kunstmuseum Luzern; Purchase 1977
Plate p. 121

Pablo Picasso
Málaga 1881 – 1973 Mougins

90
The Tree, Summer, 1907
L'Arbre
Oil on canvas, 37¹/₂ x 37¹/₄"
Musée Picasso, Paris
Plate p. 40

91
Landscape, La Rue-des-Bois, 1908
Paysage, La Rue-des-Bois
Oil on canvas, 29¹/₄ x 24"
Private collection
Plate p. 41

92
Vert-Galant, June 25, 1943
Le Vert-Galant
Oil on canvas, 25³/₄ x 36³/₄"
Musée Picasso, Paris
Plate p. 84

93
Le Déjeuner sur l'herbe, 1961
Oil on canvas, 52 x 38³/₄"
Louisiana Museum of Modern Art, Humlebæk,
Denmark; Donation: Picasso Foundation
and Louisiana Foundation
Plate p. 85

Henri Rousseau
Laval 1844 – 1910 Paris

94
The Hungry Lion Attacking an Antelope, 1905
Le Lion ayant faim se jette sur l'antilope
Oil on canvas, 78³/₄ x 118¹/₂"
Fondation Beyeler, Riehen/Basle
Plate p. 37

Egon Schiele
Tulln on the Danube 1890 – 1918 Vienna

95
Autumn Tree in a Breeze, "Autumn Tree" (III),
also *"Winter Tree"*, 1912
Herbstbaum in bewegter Luft, "Herbstbaum" (III),
auch "Winterbaum"
Oil on canvas, 32 x 32¹/₄"
Leopold Museum – Private foundation, Vienna
Plate p. 59

Chaim Soutine
Smilovichi (near Minsk) 1893 – 1943 Paris

96
The Tree of Vence, ca. 1929
L'Arbre de Vence
Oil on canvas, 32¹/₂ x 24¹/₂"
Private collection
Plate p. 71

97
Large Poplars in Civry, 1939/40
Les grands Peupliers à Civry
Oil on canvas, 29¹/₄ x 21¹/₂ '
Reuben and Edith Hecht Museum, University
of Haifa, Israel
Plate p. 73

98
Poplars, Civry, ca. 1939
Les Peupliers, Civry
Oil on canvas on wooden panel, 24¹/₂ x 13¹/₄"
Private collection
Plate p. 72

Jean Tinguely
Fribourg 1925 – 1991 Bern

99
The Bear of Bursinel, 1990
L'Ours de Bursinel
Wood, iron, vee belt, 220-V electric motors,
108³/₄ x 77¹/₂ x 88"
Museum Jean Tinguely, Basle; Donated
by Niki de Saint Phalle
Plate p. 111

Bill Viola
New York 1951

100
The Theater of Memory, 1985
Color video projection on large wall screen;
23-foot, uprooted dead tree with fifty electric
lanterns in dark room; wind chime; amplified
stereo sound, 158 x 188 x 330"
Collection of the Orange County Museum of Art,
Museum purchase
Plate pp. 128/129

Wols
Berlin 1913 – 1951 Paris

101
Trees, ca. 1946
Bäume
Oil, grattage, tube impressions on canvas,
32¹/₂ x 26"
Galerie Karsten Greve, Cologne, Paris, Milan
Plate p. 91

Oceanian Art

102
Figure of a cultural hero or creative ancestor
Biwat Group, Yuat River, Lower Sepik area,
Northeastern New Guinea, Melanesia
Wood, reddish clay sediment coating, fringed
loincloth, bone dagger; height 75$^1/_2$"
Fondation Beyeler, Riehen/Basle
Plate p. 137

103
Ancestral figure
Eastern Iatmul or southern neighbours, Central
Sepik area, including the southern tributaries
Blackwater and Korewori, Northern New Guinea,
Melanesia
Painted wood; height 53$^1/_2$"
Fondation Beyeler, Riehen/Basle
Plate p. 140

104
Hunting aide, *yipwon*
Yimar villages, Upper Korewori River, Southern
Sepik area, Northeastern New Guinea, Melanesia
Wood, cassowary feathers; height 108$^1/_4$"
Fondation Beyeler, Riehen/Basle
Plate p. 138

105
Perforated carved board figure, *malu-samban*,
Malu-"suspension hook"
Sawos or Iatmul, Central Sepik area, Northern
New Guinea, Melanesia
Wood, traces of red and white paint; height 66"
Fondation Beyeler, Riehen/Basle
Plate p. 139

106
Male figure, *nalik*, 19th century
Used for "uli" celebrations
Presumably inland of New Ireland (area of the
Mandak family of languages), Northern Melanesia
Painted wood, inlaid eyes of "Turbo petholatus"-
snail shells; height 55"
Fondation Beyeler, Riehen/Basle
Plate p. 143

107
Male figure, *nalik*, 18th/19th century
Used for "uli" celebrations
Malom, northeastern coast of New Ireland,
Melanesia
Wood, painted, partially over setting of chalk or
lime, beard of plant fibres, snail shells; height
71$^1/_2$"
Fondation Beyeler, Riehen/Basle
Plate p. 144

108
Head of a life-size *malanggan* doll, *kovabat*
(according to Gunn: "Head Rain")
Tabar Islands, New Ireland, Melanesia
Wood, painted black; height 23"
Fondation Beyeler, Riehen/Basle
Plate p. 147

109
Mask, *kepong* or *matua*
New Ireland, Melanesia
Painted wood of the Alstonia sp., printed shreds
of European cotton; height 30"
Fondation Beyeler, Riehen/Basle
Plate p. 142

110
Head of a life-size *malanggan* doll, *kovabat* (Gunn)
or *mandas* (Krämer) with bird
Presumably Lemakot, Northern New Ireland,
Melanesia
Painted wood, inlaid eyes of "Turbo petholatus"-
snail shells; height 30$^1/_4$"
Fondation Beyeler, Riehen/Basle
Plate p. 145

111
Dancing paddle, *rapa*
Easter Island (Rapa Nui)
Wood; height 30"
Fondation Beyeler, Riehen/Basle
Plate p. 141

112
Painted tree bast cloth (*tapa*), 1st half of 19th
century
Used as a gift presented on festive occasions, also
for veiling highly ranking, mana-possessing
persons and objects
Area of the Fiji islands, Western Polynesia
Pounded bast of the paper mulberry tree,
connected to obtain a large expanse, then pain-
ted; length ca. 288", width ca. 29$^1/_4$"
Museum der Kulturen, Basle
Plate pp. 148/149

113
Dugout canoe, ca. 1960
Lower Sepik area, Northern New Guinea
Wood; 266 x 13$^1/_2$ x 12"
Museum der Kulturen, Basle; Purchase
Sammlung Panzenböck, 1963

114
Supporting post of a men's and ceremonial house,
ca. 1940
Kingaui, hinterland of the Central Sepik area,
Northern New Guinea
Carved wood; height 132", diameter 200$^3/_4$"
Museum der Kulturen, Basle; Purchase
Sammlung Panzenböck, 1963

115
Standing slit gong, ca. 1960
Northern Ambrym, Vanuatu
Carved from a tree trunk; height ca. 200$^3/_4$",
diameter 13$^1/_2$ x 12"
Museum der Kulturen, Basle; Donated
by S. Jouravleff, 1997

African Art

116
Headdress, *a mantsho-na-tshol*, 19th/20th century
Form of a snake
Unknown workshop of the Baga, Nalu, Landuma,
Pukur, Bulumits regions, Guinea
Wood, painted reddish white and black; height 80"
Fondation Beyeler, Riehen/Basle
Plate p. 158

117
Pounding figure, *deble*, ca. 1870
Work of a Senufo master of the Sikasso region,
Mali
Wood with shiny dark patina; height 37$^1/_2$"
Fondation Beyeler, Riehen/Basle
Plate p. 153

118
Female reliquary figure, *biery*, 19th/20th century
Unknown Betsi master of the Southern Fang
region, Gabon
Wood with shiny dark patina; height 17$^1/_2$"
Fondation Beyeler, Riehen/Basle
Plate p. 154

119
Male ancestral figure, *lusingiti*, 19th/20th century
Unknown Hemba master of the Bena-Niembo
region, Zaire
Wood with shiny patina; height 36$^1/_2$"
Fondation Beyeler, Riehen/Basle
Plate p. 156

120
Cult figure, 19th or early 20th century
Unknown master of the Mumuye region, Nigeria
Wood with shiny dark patina; height 39"
Fondation Beyeler, Riehen/Basle
Plate p. 152

121
Nail figure, *nkisi n'konde*, before 1900
Congo workshop of the Vili region
Wood, nails and other iron fragments, cowry
shell, porcelain, resinous compound; height 41"
Fondation Beyeler, Riehen/Basle
Plate p. 155

122
Sitting figure, presumably 17th/18th century
Fragment of a slit-drum
Workshop of the M'bembe region, Nigeria
Wood (carved from a single piece), end piece of a
giant drum (ca. 80–120"); height 32", depth 21"
Fondation Beyeler, Riehen/Basle
Plate p. 157

Video documentation

Broadcast *Aspekte Extra* (Channel ZDF, 6/21/1982)
"Joseph Beuys" (7000 Oaks, documenta 7)
Length: 9'24"
documenta Archives, Kassel

Biographies

Contemporary artists

HAMISH FULTON

Born in London in 1946. Lives and works in Broad Oak, Canterbury, Kent.

One- and two-person exhibitions (selection)

1969 Konrad Fischer, Düsseldorf
1970 Gian Enzo Sperone, Torino
1971 Situation, London
1972 Gian Enzo Sperone, Torino
Art & Project, Amsterdam
Toselli, Milan
Museum of Modern Art, Oxford
Galerie Yvon Lambert, Paris
1973 Stedelijk Museum, Amsterdam
Sperone-Fischer, Rome
Art & Project – M. T. L., Antwerp
1974 Marilena Bonomo, Bari
1975 Art & Project, Amsterdam
Rolf Preisig, Basle
P. M. J. Self, London
Kunstmuseum Basel
1976 Sperone Westwater Fischer, New York
Cusak, Houston
I. C. A., London
Hester van Royen, London
Claire Copley, Los Angeles
1977 Stedelijk van Abbemuseum, Eindhoven
Robert Self, London
Sonnabend Gallery, New York
1978 Galerie Nancy Gillespie – Elisabeth de Laage, Paris
Projects, The Museum of Modern Art, New York
Centre d'Art Contemporain, Geneva
Galerie Tanit, Munich
1979 Whitechapel Art Gallery, London
Art & Project, Amsterdam
1980 Galerie Gillespie-Laage-Salomon, Paris
Thackry & Robertson, San Francisco
Graeme Murray, Edinburgh
Kanransha Gallery, Tokyo
Waddington Galleries, London
1981 Massimo Valsecchi, Milan
Centre Georges Pompidou, Paris
1982 Orchard Gallery, Londonderry
1983 Galerie Gillespie-Laage-Salomon, Paris
John Weber Gallery, New York
1984 Centre d'Art Contemporain, Geneva
1985 *Hamish Fulton 1975 - 85*, Stedelijk Van Abbe-museum, Eindhoven; Nouveau Musée, Villeur-banne; Fruitmarket Gallery, Edinburgh; Mendel Art Gallery, Saskatoon, Canada
Castello di Rivoli (with Ulay and Marina Abramović)
1986 Victoria Miro Gallery, London
Galerij S 65, Aalst, Belgium
Cairn Gallery, Nailsworth, Great Britain
1987 Galerij S 65, Aalst, Belgium

1988 Domaine de Kerguehennec, Centre d'Art Contemporain, Locminé, France
Temple University, Philadelphia
Gallery Senda, Hiroshima
1989 *Here and There Travels*, Clocktower Gallery, New York
1990 *Selected Walks 1969 - 1989*, Albright-Knox Art Gallery, Buffalo
National Gallery of Canada, Ottawa
El Centro Cultural/Arte Contemporaneo, Mexico City
Musée de Grenoble, France
Galerie Laage-Salomon, Paris
1991 Galerie Tanit, Cologne
Marika Malacorda, Geneva
Serpentine Gallery, London
Haags Gemeentemuseum, the Hague
1992 Staatliche Kunsthalle, Baden-Baden
Abbaye de Saint Savin, France
Galleri Riis, Oslo
Ivam Centre Julio González, Valencia
1993 Annely Juda Fine Art, London
Galleria Massimo Minini, Brescia
Galerie Laage-Salomon, Paris
1994 Galerie Lydie Rekow, Crest, France
Luis Serpa, Lisbon
1995 Centre d'Art Contemporain, Geneva
Galerie Tschudi, Glarus, Switzerland
Lenbachhaus, Munich
1996 Önnur hæð, Second Floor, Reykjavík
Musée de Valence, France
Museum of Modern Art, Wakayama, Japan (with Roger Ackling)
Galerie Stadtpark, Krems, Austria
Galerie Artek, Helsinki
Olga Korper Gallery, Toronto
1997 Galerie Mueller-Roth, Stuttgart
Texas Gallery, Houston
The Art Museum of Missoula, Montana
1998 *Walking beside the River Vechte*, Städtische Galerie Nordhorn, Germany
Kunstverein Düsseldorf (with Peter Hutchinson)
Koyanagi Gallery, Tokyo, Japan

RODNEY GRAHAM

Born in Vancouver in 1949. Lives and works in Vancouver.

One- and two-person exhibitions (selection)

1976 Pender Street Gallery, Vancouver (with Robert Kleyn)
1979 *Camera Obscura*, Abbotsford, Canada
Illuminated Ravine, Simon Fraser University, Burnady
1986 Galerie Johnen & Schöttle, Cologne

1987 Art Gallery of Ontario, Toronto
Coburg Gallery, Vancouver (with James Welling)
Ydessa Gallery, Toronto
1988 Philip Nelson, Lyons
Galerie Johnen & Schöttle, Cologne
Vancouver Art Gallery (cat.)
1989 Galerie Micheline Szwajcer, Antwerp
Books and Writings by Rodney Graham, Yves Gevaert, Brussels
Galería Marga Paz, Madrid
Stedelijk Van Abbemuseum, Eindhoven (cat.)
1990 *Parsifal*, Galerie Johnen & Schöttle, Cologne
Galerie Rüdiger Schöttle, Munich (with Ian Wallace)
Christine Burgin Gallery, New York
Books, Lisson Gallery, London
1991 Maison de la Culture et de la Communication de Saint-Etienne
1992 Galerie Nelson, Lyons (with Ken Lum)
Galerie Rüdiger Schöttle, Paris
1993 Galerie Micheline Szwajcer, Antwerp (cat.)
Lisson Gallery, London
1993/94: Angles Gallery, Santa Monica
1994 Art Gallery of York University, North York
Rodney Graham. Works from the Permanent Collection, Art Metropole, Ontario
Office of Bernhard Starkmann, Boston
303 Gallery, New York
1995 Fundació Espai Poblenou, Barcelona
The Renaissance Society, Chicago
Galerie Johnen & Schöttle, Cologne
Musée départemental d'art contemporain de Rochechouart, France
1995/96: Galerie Rüdiger Schöttle, Munich
1996 FRAC de Haute Normandie, Rouen
Nicole Klagsbrun, New York
Morris and Helen Belkin Art Gallery, Vancouver
1996/97: Lisson Gallery, London
1997 XLVIIth Biennale, Venice, Canadian Pavilion (cat.)
303 Gallery, New York
Angles Gallery, Los Angeles
1998 Galerie Rüdiger Schöttle, Munich (with Stephan Balkenhol)

Group exhibitions (selection)

1973 *Pacific Vibrations*, Vancouver Art Gallery
1976 *Eight West Coast Artists*, Pender Street Gallery, Vancouver
1979 *Local Colour*, Nova Gallery, Vancouver
1980 *Critics Choice*, Hal Bromm Gallery, New York
1984 *Poco Rococo*, Port Coquitlam Mall, Port Coquitlam, Canada
1985 *Rodney Graham, Ken Lum, Jeff Wall, Ian Wallace*, 49th Parallel Centre for Contemporary Canadian Art, New York (cat.)

Barbara Ess, Rodney Graham, Ken Lum, Galerie Rüdiger Schöttle, Munich
Thought Objects, Cash/Newhouse Gallery, New York
1986 *Ricochet*, Sala 1, Rome (cat.)
Fokus. Canada 1960-1985, Art Cologne, 20. Internationaler Kunstmarkt Köln, Rheinhallen, Messegelände, Cologne
1987 *Skulptur. Projekte Münster*, Westfälisches Landesmuseum für Kunst und Kulturgeschichte, Münster (cat.)
Cinema Objects, De Appel Foundation, Amsterdam
Dan Graham, Rodney Graham, Robert Smithson, Jeff Wall, Christine Burgin Gallery, New York
Non in codice, Galleria Mario Pieroni, Rome, and The American Academy in Rome (cat.)
1988 *Drawings*, Cable Gallery, New York
Essential Form, Walter Philips Gallery, Banff, Canada (cat.)
Facsimile, De Zaak, Groningen (cat.)
Made in Camera, Galleri Sten Eriksson, Stockholm (cat.)
1989 Ralph Wernicke, Stuttgart
Bestiarium. Jardin-théatre, Entrepôt-Galerie de Confort Moderne, Poitiers (cat.)
Casino de la Exposición, Seville
1990 *Hacia el paisaje*, Centro Atlantico de Arte Moderna, Las Palmas de Gran Canaria (cat.)
Centre International d'Art Contemporain, Montreal
Real Allegories, Lisson Gallery, London
1990/91: *Weitersehen*, Museum Haus Esters and Museum Haus Lange, Krefeld (cat.)
1990/91: S. L. Simpson Gallery, Toronto
1990/91: *Le Diaphane. Une réflexion, une collection, une exposition, un lieu*, Musée des Beaux-Arts and Ecole des Beaux-Arts, Tourcoing, France
1991 *Vanitas*, Galerie Crousel-Robelin/Bama, Paris
Nieuwe vieugel, Stedelijk Van Abbemuseum, Eindhoven
Crossroads, Art Gallery of York University, North York (cat.)
Lost Illusions, Vancouver Art Gallery
1992 *La Revanche de l'image*, Galerie Pierre Huber, Geneva (cat.)
Cameres indiscretes, Centre d'Art Santa Monica, Barcelona (cat.)
Teatrojardin. Bestiarium, Casino de la Exposición, Seville (cat.)
DOCUMENTA IX, Kassel (cat.)
Stars don't stand still in the sky. Hommage à Stéphane Mallarmé, Kunstmuseum Winterthur, Switzerland
The Binary Era. New Interactions, Musée Communal d'Ixelles; also travelled to Vienna and Japan (cat.)
Inscapes, De Appel, Amsterdam (cat.)
Books, Prints, Objects, Stedelijk Van Abbemuseum, Eindhoven (cat.)
Acquisitions. 1989-1993, Stedelijk Van Abbemuseum, Eindhoven (cat.)
1993 *Canada. Une nouvelle génération*, Musée municipal, La-Roche-sur-Yon
Binaera. 14 Interaktionen: Kunst und Technologie, Kunsthalle Wien

Voyage to Cythera, Palazzo Vendramin-Calergi, XLVth Biennale, Venice
Galerie Johnen & Schöttle, Cologne
Corners filled with what is swept into corners, Galerie Micheline Szwajcer, Antwerp (cat.)
1994 *Beeld - Beeld*, Museum van Hedendaagse Kunst, Citadelpark, Genth
Serial, Angles Gallery, Santa Monica
Des objets sans fondation, Résidence Secondaire, Carrée Saint Nicholas, Paris
1995 Centre Genevois de Gravure Contemporaine, Geneva
About the Place. Recent Art in the Americas, The Art Institute of Chicago
Les Fragments du désir, Futur Musée des Instruments, Brussels
Artistes - Architects, Nouveau Musée, Institut d'Art Contemporain, Villeurbanne
Spirits at the Crossing, Setagaya Art Museum, Tokyo; The National Museum of Modern Art, Kyoto; Hokkaido Museum of Modern Art, Sapporo
1996 Galerie Johnen & Schöttle, Cologne
Lesen!, Kunsthalle Sankt Gallen (cat.)
The Architecture of Dreams, Museo Regional de Guadalajara
Topographies, Vancouver Art Gallery
The Culture of Nature, Kamloops Art Gallery, Canada
Rodney Graham, Geoffry James, Richard Long, Angles Gallery, Los Angeles
1997 *Sites of the Visual*, Art Gallery of Windsor, Canada (cat.)
Patrick Painter Editions, S. L. Simpson Gallery, Toronto
Niemandsland, Krefelder Kunstmuseen
1998 *From Here to There*, Fundaçao Calouste Gulbenkian, Lisbon
Projected Allegories, Contemporary Arts Museum, Houston
Then And Now, Lisson Gallery, London
A Sense of Place, Angles Gallery, Santa Monica

WOLFGANG LAIB

Born in 1950 in Metzingen. Lives and works in Southern Germany

One- and two-person exhibitions (selection)

1976 Galerie Mueller-Roth, Stuttgart
1978 Galleria Salvatore Ala, Milan
Konrad Fischer, Düsseldorf
Rolf Preisig, Basle
Kunstraum München
1979 Sperone Westwater Fischer, New York
Kabinett für aktuelle Kunst, Bremerhaven
Jean & Karen Bernier, Athens
1981 Sperone Westwater Fischer, New York
Kabinett für aktuelle Kunst, Bremerhaven
Galerie Max Hetzler, Stuttgart
Galerie Crousel-Hussenot, Paris
1982 Gewad, Genth
Konrad Fischer, Zurich
1983 Städtisches Museum Abteiberg, Mönchengladbach
Konrad Fischer, Düsseldorf

1984 Kabinett für aktuelle Kunst, Bremerhaven
1985 Kunstverein St. Gallen
Whitechapel Art Gallery, London
1986 ARC, Musée d'Art Moderne de la Ville de Paris
Galerie Maeght Lelong, New York
Galerie Crousel-Hussenot, Paris
capc Musée d'Art Contemporain, Bordeaux
1987 Galerie Buchmann, Basle
1988 Ruine der Künste, Berlin
Lelong, New York
Des Moines Art Center
Burnett Miller Gallery, Los Angeles
1989 Musée départemental d'art contemporain de Rochechouart
Fundació Joan Miró, Barcelona
Galerie Buchmann, Basle
Galerie Crousel-Robelin/Bama, Paris
Württembergischer Kunstverein, Stuttgart
1990 Kabinett für aktuelle Kunst, Bremerhaven
Galerie Buchmann, Basle
Galerie des Beaux-Arts, Brussels
Kunstmuseum Luzern
Konrad Fischer, Düsseldorf
Burnett Miller Gallery, Los Angeles
Rhona Hoffmann Gallery, Chicago
1991 Sperone Westwater, New York
Senda Gallery, Hiroshima
Galerie Buchmann, Basle
Kanransha Gallery, Tokyo
Galerie Crousel-Robelin/Bama, Paris
Center for Contemporary Arts, Santa Fe
1992 Centre Georges Pompidou, Musée national d'art moderne, Paris
Artiaco Galleria, Naples
Museo Comunale d'Arte Moderna di Ascona
The Douglas Hyde Gallery, Dublin
Kunstmuseum Bern
capc Musée d'Art Contemporain, Bordeaux
MOCA, Museum of Contemporary Art, Los Angeles
1993 Sperone Westwater, New York
De Pont stichting voor hedendaagse kunst, Tilburg
Galerie Buchmann, Basle
1993 The Henry Moore Sculpture Trust Studio, Halifax, Great Britain
Galerie Thaddäus Ropac, Salzburg
Camden Arts Centre, London
1995 Installation in the Sprengel Museum Hannover
Sperone Westwater, New York
1996 Konrad Fischer, Düsseldorf
Galerie Thaddäus Ropac, Salzburg
Galerie Artek, Helsinki
Galerie Chantal Crousel, Paris
Kenji Taki Gallery, Nagoya
1997 Kenji Taki Gallery, Nagoya
Staatliche Kunsthalle, Karlsruhe
1998 The Arts Club of Chicago
Sperone Westwater, New York
Kenji Taki Gallery, Nagoya and Tokyo

Group exhibitions (selection)

1980 1st exhibition of the Jürgen Ponto-Stiftung, Carmelite cloister, Frankfort
InK, Zurich (with Brice Marden, Gerhard Merz, and Gilberto Zorio)

1981 *Art Allemagne Aujord'hui*, ARC, Musée d'Art
Moderne de la Ville de Paris
Annemarie und Will Grohmann-Stipendium,
Staatliche Kunsthalle Baden-Baden
1982 *documenta 7*, Kassel
XLth Biennale, Venice, German Pavilion (with
H. Darboven and G. Graubner)
Kunst wird Material, Nationalgalerie, Berlin
1983 *Materie + Form*, ETH, Zurich
*Kosmische Bilder in der Kunst des 20. Jahrhun-
derts*, Staatliche Kunsthalle Baden-Baden; Tel
Aviv Museum of Art
1985 *1945 bis 1985. Kunst in der Bundesrepublik
Deutschland*, Nationalgalerie, Berlin
East West Visual Arts Encounters, Jehangir Art
Gallery, Bombay
*Spuren, Skulpturen und Monumente ihrer
präzisen Reise*, Kunsthaus Zürich
1986 *Ouverture II*, Castello di Rivoli
Falls the Shadow. The Hayward Annual,
Hayward Gallery, London
VI. Biennale of Sydney, Art Gallery of New
South Wales, Sydney
De Sculptura, Messepalast, Vienna
SkulpturSein, Städtische Kunsthalle
Düsseldorf
1987 *Wechselströme*, Bonner Kunstverein
documenta 8, Kassel
Century 87, Oude Kerk, Amsterdam
1988 *Zeitlos*, Hamburger Bahnhof, Berlin
Rosc, Dublin
Carnegie International 88, The Carnegie
Museum of Art, Pittsburgh
1989 *Hortus Artis*, Orto Botanico, Torino
Color and/or Monochrome, The National
Museum of Modern Art, Tokyo; The National
Museum of Modern Art, Kyoto
Glanzlichter, Städtisches Kunstmuseum Bonn
Einleuchten, Deichtorhallen, Hamburg
Museum of Contemporary Art, Chicago (with
Gerhard Merz and Franz Erhard Walther)
1990 *Treshold*, The National Museum of Contempo-
rary Art, Oslo
Signs of Life, Institute of Contemporary Art,
Philadelphia
LightSeed, The Watari Museum of Contempo-
rary Art, Tokyo (with Cy Twombly and Michel
Verjux)
1991 *Das Goldene Zeitalter*, Württembergischer
Kunstverein, Stuttgart
1992 *Vorhut aus dem Hinterland*, Neues Museum
Weserburg Bremen
Territorium Artis, Kunst- und Ausstellungs-
halle der Bundesrepublik Deutschland, Bonn
De Opening, De Pont stichting voor heden-
daagse kunst, Tilburg
1993 *GAS, Grandiose Ambitieux Silencieux*, capc
Musée d'Art Contemporain, Bordeaux
Das 21. Jahrhundert, Kunsthalle Basel
*Les Pensées bleues. Baselitz, Cucchi, Laib, Paik,
Raynaud*, capc Musée d'Art Contemporain,
Bordeaux
1994 *Figur - Natur*, Sprengel Museum Hannover
Entre le ciel et l'eau, Lenbachhaus, Munich;
1995: capc Musée d'Art Contemporain,
Bordeaux
1995 *Kunst in Deutschland*, Kunst- und
Ausstellungshalle der Bundesrepublik
Deutschland, Bonn

1996 Casa-Museo Luis Barragán, Mexico City
Spirit and Place, Museum of Contemporary
Art, Sydney
1997 *Epicenter Ljubljana*, Moderna Galerija,
Ljubljana
Still Life, The Museum of Modern Art, New
York
XLVIIth Biennale, Venice
Biennale de Lyon, Lyons
Biennale Kwangju, Corea
1998 *Geistes Gegenwart*, Diözesanmuseum Freising,
Germany
Orientalismos, KM Kulturunea, San Sebastian
Etre nature, Fondation Cartier pour l'Art con-
temporain, Paris

RICHARD LONG

Born in Bristol in 1946. Lives and works in Bristol.

One- and two-person exhibitions (selection)

1968 Konrad Fischer, Düsseldorf
1969 Museum Haus Lange, Krefeld (cat.)
1970 Städtisches Museum Abteiberg, Mönchengladbach (cat.)
Dwan Gallery, New York
1971 Art & Project, Amsterdam
Museum of Modern Art, Oxford
1972 *Projects. Richard Long*, The Museum of
Modern Art, New York
1973 Lisson Gallery, London
Stedelijk Museum, Amsterdam (cat.)
1974 John Weber Gallery, New York
Inca Rock Campfire Ash, Scottish National
Gallery of Modern Art, Edinburgh (cat.)
1975 *Richard Long. Driftwood*, Wide White Space,
Antwerp
Rolf Preisig, Basle
1976 Konrad Fischer, Düsseldorf
Sperone Westwater Fischer, New York
1977 *A Hundred Stones*, Kunsthalle Bern (cat.)
National Gallery of Victoria, Melbourne
Richard Long. John Kaldor Art Project 6, Art
Gallery of New South Wales, Sydney (cat.)
1978 *Driftwood Circle*, Art & Project, Amsterdam
InK, Halle für internationale neue Kunst,
Zurich
Ausstellungsraum Ulrich Rückriem,
Hamburg
1979 *The River Avon*, Anthony d'Offay Gallery,
London
Richard Long. Sculpturen en Fotowerken,
Stedelijk Van Abbemuseum, Eindhoven (cat.)
1980 *Richard Long. Stone Circles*, Jean & Karen
Bernier, Athens
Richard Long. Stones and Sticks, Art & Project,
Amsterdam (cat.)
Fogg Art Museum, Harvard University,
Cambridge (cat.)
1981 Anthony d'Offay Gallery, London (cat.)
capc Musée d'Art Contemporain, Bordeaux
1982 Art & Project, Amsterdam (cat.)
National Gallery of Canada, Ottawa (cat.)
1983 *Richard Long. Selected Works*, Arnolfini Bristol
Gallery (cat.)
Century Cultural Center, Tokyo (cat.)

1984 *Richard Long. Stone*, Galleria Lucio Amelio,
Naples
Concentrations 9. Richard Long, Dallas
Museum of Art (cat.)
Orchard Gallery, Londonderry (cat.)
1985 Galerie Buchmann, Basle (cat.)
Malmö Konsthall (cat.)
1986 *Piedras. Richard Long*, Palacio de Cristal (cat.)
Solomon R. Guggenheim Museum, New York
1987 Musée Rath, Geneva (cat.)
Donald Young Gallery, Chicago (cat.)
1988 Konrad Fischer, Düsseldorf
3. Kunstpreis Aachen. Richard Long, Neue
Galerie – Sammlung Ludwig, Aachen (cat.)
1989 Kunstverein St. Gallen (cat.)
La Jolla Museum of Contemporary Art,
California (cat.)
1990 Anthony d'Offay Gallery, London (cat.)
Galerie Tschudi, Glarus, Switzerland
Tate Gallery, London (cat.)
Musée départemental d'art contemporain de
Rochechouart (cat.)
1991 Weber, Alexander y Cobo, Madrid (with
Hamish Fulton)
Tate Gallery Liverpool (cat.)
Städtische Galerie im Städelschen Kunst-
institut, Frankfort (cat.)
Richard Long. Walking in Cercles, Hayward
Gallery, London (cat.)
1992 Meadow gallery, University of Warwick
1993 ARC, Musée d'Art Moderne de la Ville de
Paris
Center of Contemporary Arts, Santa Fe
Neues Museum Weserburg Bremen
1994 Kunstsammlung Nordrhein-Westfalen,
Düsseldorf
Philadelphia Museum of Art
Bienal de São Paulo, São Paulo
Museum of Contemporary Art, Sydney
1995 Bündner Kunstverein and Bündner Kunst-
museum, Chur
Peter Blum, New York
Önnur hæð, Second Floor, Reykjavík
1996 Setagaya Art Museum, Tokyo
Contemporary Arts Museum, Houston
Modern Art Museum of Fort Worth
1997 Wilhelm Lehmbruck Museum Duisburg
Benesse House Naoshima, Contemporary Art
Museum, Japan
Kunst auf der Zugspitze, Zugspitze, Germany

Group exhibitions (selection)

1967 *19:45 – 21:55*, Dorothea Loehr, Frankfurt
1968 *Young Contemporaries*, Royal Institute
Galleries, London
A3. Arte e azione povera, Amalfi
1969 *Earth Art*, Andrew Dickson White Museum of
Art, Cornell University, Ithaca, N.Y.
*Op losse schroeven. Situaties en cryptostruc-
turen*, Stedelijk Museum, Amsterdam
When Attitudes Become Form, Kunsthalle
Bern
1970 *Information*, The Museum of Modern Art,
New York
1971 *Sonsbeek 71*, Park Sonsbeek, Arnheim
1972 *documenta 5*, Kassel
The New Art, Hayward Gallery, London

1974 *C. Andre, M. Broodthaers, D. Buren, V. Burgin, Gilbert & George, On Kawara, R. Long, G. Richter*, Palais des Beaux-Arts, Brussels
1975 *Artists Over Land*, Arnolfini Bristol Gallery
1976 *Andre, LeVa, Long*, The Corcoran Gallery of Art, Washington
1977 *M. Asher, D. Askevold, R. Long*, Los Angeles Institute of Contemporary Art
   Skulptur, Westfälisches Landesmuseum für Kunst und Kulturgeschichte, Münster
1979 *Skulptur. Matisse, Giacometti, Judd, Flavin, Andre, Long*, Kunsthalle Bern
1980 *Andre, Dibbets, Long, Ryman*, Louisiana Museum for Moderne Kunst, Humlebæk
   Pier + Ocean. Construction in the Art of the Seventies, Hayward Gallery, London
1981 *British Sculpture in the 20th Century. Part 2: Symbol and Imagination 1951-1980*, Whitechapel Art Gallery, London
1982 *documenta 7*, Kassel
1984 *›Primitivism‹ in 20th Century Art*, The Museum of Modern Art, New York
1985 *Ouverture. Arte contemporanea*, Castello di Rivoli
1986 *Falls the Shadow. Recent British and European Art. 1986*, Hayward Gallery, London
1987 *British Art in the 20th Century. The Modern Movement*, Royal Academy of Art, London
1988 *Donald Judd, Richard Long, Kristján Gudmundsson*, Nylistasafnid, The Living Art Museum, Reykjavík
1989 *Magiciens de la terre*, Centre Georges Pompidou and Grande Halle – La Villette, Paris
   2. Istanbul Bienali, Süleymaniye Imaret, Istanbul
1991 *Den Gedanken auf der Spur bleiben*, Museum Haus Esters and Museum Haus Lange, Krefeld
1992 *Sculpture in the Close*, Jesus College, Cambridge
1993 *Gravity and Grace*, Hayward Gallery, London
   Feuer, Wasser, Erde, Luft. Die Vier Elemente, Deichtorhallen, Hamburg
1994 Philadelphia Museum of Art
   Mapping, The Museum of Modern Art, New York
1995 *Drawing the Line*, Southampton City Art Gallery
1996 *Une siècle de sculpture anglaise*, Jeu de Paume, Paris
   Abstraction in the 20th Century. Total Risk, Freedom, Discipline, The Solomon R. Guggenheim Museum, New York

GIUSEPPE PENONE

Born in Garessio in 1947. Lives and works in Torino.

One- and two-person exhibitions (selection)

1968 Deposito d'arte presente, Torino (cat.)
1969 Gian Enzo Sperone, Torino
1970 Aktionsraum I, Munich (cat.)
   Toselli, Milan
1972 Galerie Paul Maenz, Cologne
1973 Multipli, Torino
   Sperone-Fischer, Rome

1974 Schema, Florence
   Galerie 'T Venster, Rotterdam
1975 Samangallery, Genoa
   Sperone Gallery, New York
1976 Studio De Ambrogi, Milan
1977 *Bäume Augen Haare Wände Tongefäss*, Kunstmuseum Luzern (cat.)
1978 Staatliche Kunsthalle Baden-Baden (cat.)
   Galleria Salvatore Ala, Milan 1978
1979 Liliane & Michel Durand-Dessert, Paris
   1979/80: Halle für internationale neue Kunst, Zurich
1980 Stedelijk Museum, Amsterdam (cat.)
   Halle für internationale neue Kunst, Zurich
   Lisson Gallery, London
1981 *Essere fiume*, Konrad Fischer, Düsseldorf
1982 Städtisches Museum Abteiberg, Mönchengladbach (cat.)
1983 National Gallery of Canada, Ottawa
   Museum of Contemporary Art, Chicago (cat.)
1984 ARC, Musée d'Art Moderne de la Ville de Paris (cat.)
1985 Marian Goodman Gallery, New York
   Château de Malle, Preignac (cat.)
1986 Musée de Peinture et Sculpture, Grenoble (cat.)
   Neue Arbeiten, Galerie Buchmann, Basle (cat.)
   Musée des Beaux-Art, Nantes (cat.)
1987 Musée Rodin, Paris
1989 *Recent Sculpture*, Dean Clough Art Foundation, Halifax, Great Britain
   Six Weeks of Sculpture, Arnolfini Bristol Gallery
   1989/90: Galleria d'Arte Moderna, Villa delle Rose, Bologna (cat.)
1991 *Folgie e Suture*, Eglise de Courmelois, Val-De-Vesle (cat.)
   1991/92: Castello di Rivoli (cat.)
1992 *Raccogliere gli sguardi*, Galerie Jule Kewenig, Frechen
   Giuseppe Penone invita Johannes Cladders, Foro per l'Arte contemporanea, Scavi archeologici, Verona (cat.)
1993 Musée-Château d'Annecy (cat.)
1994 *Giuseppe Penone. L'Image du toucher*, Maison de la Culture d'Amiens and FRAC Picardie, Amiens (cat.)
1996 Galerie Paul Andriesse, Amsterdam
1997 *Die Adern des Steins*, Kunstmuseum Bonn and Toyota Municipal Museum of Art (cat.)
   Pièges de lumière, Carée d'Art, Musée d'Art Contemporain, Nîmes
1998 Galleria Civica d'Arte Contemporanea, Trent
   Konrad Fischer, Düsseldorf

Group exhibitions (selection)

1969 *Prospekt 69*, Städtische Kunsthalle Düsseldorf (cat.)
1970 Fukuoka Prefectural Culture House (cat.)
   Processi di pensiero visualizzati. Kunstmuseum Luzern (cat.)
   Conceptual Art, Arte Povera, Land Art, Galleria Civica d'Arte Moderna, Torino (cat.)
1971 *Arte Povera. 13 italienische Künstler*, Kunstverein München (cat.)
1972 *documenta 5*, Kassel (cat.)

1974 *Die verlorene Identität. Zur Gegenwart des Romantischen*, Städtisches Museum Leverkusen (cat.)
   Kunst bleibt Kunst. Projekt '74, Josef-Haubrich-Kunsthalle and Kölnischer Kunstverein Cologne (cat.)
1975 *XIII Bienal de São Paulo*, Museo de Arte Moderna, São Paulo
1976 *The 1976 Biennale of Sydney*, The Art Gallery of New South Wales (cat.)
1978 *Dall'arte alla natura, dalla natura all'arte*, XXXVIIIth Biennale, Venice (cat.)
1980 *L'arte negli anni '70*, XXXIXth Biennale, Venice
1981 *Westkunst*, Rheinhallen, Messegelände, Cologne (cat.)
   Identité italienne. L'Art en Italie depuis 1959, Centre Georges Pompidou, Musée national d'art moderne, Paris (cat.)
1982 *Italian Art Now. An American Perspective. 1982*, Solomon R. Guggenheim Museum, New York (cat.)
   documenta 7, Kassel (cat.)
1983 *De statua*, Stedelijk Van Abbemuseum, Eindhoven (cat.)
   Biennale 17, Middelheim, Antwerp (cat.)
1984 *Il Modo Italiano*, Fischer Gallery, University of Southern California, Los Angeles (cat.)
   An International Survey of Recent Painting and Sculpture, The Museum of Modern Art, New York (cat.)
   Skulptur im 20. Jahrhundert, Merian Park, Basle (cat.)
1985 *The European Iceberg*, Art Gallery of Ontario, Toronto (cat.)
   Ouverture. Arte contemporanea, Castello di Rivoli (cat.)
1986 *Sonsbeek '86*, Arnheim (cat.)
   Wunderkammern, XLIInd Biennale, Venice (cat.)
   Beuys zu Ehren, Städtische Galerie im Lenbachhaus, Munich (cat.)
1987 *Skulptur. Projekte Münster*, Westfälisches Landesmuseum für Kunst und Kulturgeschichte, Münster (cat.)
   documenta 8, Kassel (cat.)
1988 *Mythos Italien*, Bayerische Staatsgemäldesammlungen, Munich (cat.)
   Zurück zur Natur, aber wie?, Städtische Galerie im Prinz-Max-Palais, Karlsruhe (cat.)
   From the Southern Cross, VII. Biennale of Sydney, Art Gallery of New South Wales (cat.)
1989 *Italian Art in the Twentieth Century*, Royal Academy of Art, London (cat.)
   2000 Jahre. Die Gegenwart der Vergangenheit, Bonner Kunstverein (cat.)
1990 *Von der Natur in der Kunst*, Wiener Festwochen, Vienna (cat.)
   Temperamenti. Contemporary Art from Northern Italy, Tramway, Glasgow (cat.)
1991 *Arte Povera 1971 und 20 Jahre danach*, Kunstverein München (cat.)
   Il miraggio della liricità. Arte astratta in Italia dal dopoguerra ad oggi, Liljevalchs Konsthall, Stockholm (cat.)
1992 *Pour la suite du monde*, Musée d'art contemporain de Montreal (cat.)
1993 *Un'avventura internazionale, Torino e le arti 1950-1970*, Castello di Rivoli (cat.)

10 ans - 10 œuvres, FRAC Picardie, Amiens (cat.)
Manifeste. Arte Povera, Centre Georges Pompidou, Musée national d'art moderne, Paris (cat.)
1994 *The Italian Metamorphosis 1943-1968*, Solomon R. Guggenheim Museum, New York (cat.)
Prospekt - Retrospect, Kunstmuseum Luzern (cat.)
L'orizzonte. Capalavori delle Stedelijk Museum di Amsterdam, Castello di Rivoli
1995 XLVIth Biennale, Venice (cat.)
Féminin - Masculin. Le Sexe de l'art, Centre Georges Pompidou, Musée national d'art moderne, Paris (cat.)
Time Machine. Antico Egitto e arte contemporanea, Museo Egizio, Torino (cat.)
1996 *L'Art du corps*, MAC, Galeries contemporaines des musées de Marseille (cat.)
1996/97: *New Persona - New Universe*, Biennale di Firenze, Stazione Leopolda, Florence (cat.)
1997 *Arte Povera. Die Sammlung Goetz*, Neues Museum Weserburg Bremen
Images du corps, Maison de la Culture de la Province de Namur
1997/98: *Italian Art 1945-1995. The Visible and the Invisible*, Aichi Prefectural Museum of Art, Japan
1998 *Arte città. 11 artisti per il passante ferroviario di Torino*, Galleria Civica d'Arte Moderna et Contemporanea, Torino
Jardin d'artiste. De Mémoire d'arbre, Musée Zadkine, Paris
Etre nature, Fondation Cartier pour l'Art contemporain, Paris

BILL VIOLA

Born in New York in 1951. Lives and works in Long Beach, California.

One- and two-person exhibitions (selection)

1973 *New Video Work*, Everson Museum of Art, Syracuse
1974 *Bill Viola. Video and Sound Installations*, The Kitchen Center, New York
1975 *Rain. Three Interlocking Systems*, Everson Museum of Art, Syracuse
1977 The Kitchen Center, New York
1979 *Projects. Bill Viola*, The Museum of Modern Art, New York
1980 Long Beach Museum of Art
1981 Vancouver Art Gallery
1982 Whitney Museum of American Art, New York
1983 ARC, Musée d'Art Moderne de la Ville de Paris
1985 Moderna Museet, Stockholm
1987 *Bill Viola. Installations and Videotapes*, The Museum of Modern Art, New York
1988 *Bill Viola. Survey of a Decade*, Contemporary Arts Museum, Houston
1989 *Bill Viola*, Fukui Prefectural Museum of Art, The 3rd Fukui International Video Biennale, Fukui City, Japan

1990 *Bill Viola. The Sleep of Reason*, Fondation Cartier pour l'Art contemporain, Jouy-en-Josas, France
1992 *Bill Viola. Slowly Turning Narrative*, organised by the Institute of Contemporary Art, University of Pennsylvania, Philadelphia, and the Virginia Museum of Fine Arts, Richmond
Bill Viola. Unseen Images, Städtische Kunsthalle Düsseldorf; 1993: Moderna Museet, Stockholm; Museo Nacional Centro de Arte Reina Sofía, Madrid; Musée Cantonal des Beaux-Arts, Lausanne; Whitechapel Art Gallery, London; 1994: Tel Aviv Museum of Art
1993 Musée d'art contemporain de Montreal
1994 *Bill Viola. Território do Invisível/Site of the Unseen*, Centro Cultural, Banco do Brasil, Rio de Janeiro
Salzburger Kunstverein
Bill Viola. Images and Spaces, Madison Art Center
1995 *Bill Viola. Stations*, Stedelijk Van Abbemuseum, Eindhoven
1997 *Bill Viola*, Whitney Museum of American Art, New York; Los Angeles County Museum of Art; 1998: Stedelijk Museum, Amsterdam (cat.)
1998 *Bill Viola. The Messenger*, Krannert Art Museum, University of Illinois, Champaign; Melbourne Festival

Special performance

1994 *Wien Modern*, premiere of the 35-mm film *Déserts* accompanied by a live performance of Edgar Varèse's composition *Déserts* by the Ensemble Modern, conducted by Peter Eötvös, oct. 23, Konzerthaus, Vienna

Group exhibitions (selection)

1972 *St. Jude Invitational Exhibition*, De Saisset Art Gallery and Museum, Santa Clara
1975-77 *La Biennale de Paris*, ARC, Musée d'Art Moderne de la Ville de Paris
1975-87 and 1993 All *Biennial Exhibitions*, Whitney Museum of American Art, New York
1976 *Beyond the Artist's Hand. Explorations of Change*, Art Gallery, California State University, Long Beach
1977 *documenta 6*, Kassel
1978 *International Open Encounter on Video, Tokyo '78*, Tokyo
1979 *Everson Video Review*, Everson Museum of Art, Syracuse
1981 *International Video Art Festival. Portopia '81*, Theme Pavilion, Kobe, Japan
1982 *'60 - '80. Attitudes/Concepts/Images*, Stedelijk Museum, Amsterdam
1983 *Video as Attitude*, Museum of Fine Arts, Santa Fe
1984 *The Luminous Image*, Stedelijk Museum, Amsterdam
1985 *Currents*, The Institute of Contemporary Art, Boston
1986 XLIInd Biennale, Venice
1987 *Avant-Garde in the Eighties*, Los Angeles County Museum of Art

1988 *Carnegie International*, The Carnegie Museum of Art, Pittsburgh
1989 *Einleuchten*, Deichtorhallen, Hamburg
Image World, Art and Media Culture, Whitney Museum of American Art, New York
1990 *Passages de l'image*, Centre Georges Pompidou, Musée national d'art moderne, Paris; 1991: Centre Culturel Fundació Caixa de Pensions, Barcelona; Wexner Art Center, Columbus; 1992: San Francisco Museum of Modern Art
1991 *Metropolis*, Martin-Gropius-Bau, Berlin
Inaugural exhibition, Museum für Moderne Kunst, Frankfort
1992 *Pour la suite du monde*, Musée d'art contemporain de Montreal
DOCUMENTA IX, Kassel
1993 *New World Images*, Louisiana Museum for Moderne Kunst, Humlebæk
American Art in the 20th Century, Martin-Gropius-Bau, Berlin; Royal Academy of Arts and Saatchi Gallery, London
1994 *Beeld - Beeld*, Museum van Hedendaagse Kunst, Citadelpark, Genth
Landscape as Metaphor, Denver Art Museum; Columbus Museum of Art
1995 *MultiMediale 4*, Zentrum für Kunst und Medientechnologie Karlsruhe
Video Spaces. Eight Installations, The Museum of Modern Art, New York
Rites of Passage, Tate Gallery, London
Buried Secrets, XLVIth Biennale, Venice, Pavilion of the United States; Kestner-Gesellschaft, Hanover; 1996: Arizona State University Art Museum, Tempe
3e Biennale d'art contemporain de Lyon, Musée d'art contemporain, Lyons
1996 *By Night*, Fondation Cartier pour l'Art contemporain, Paris
Portrait of the Artist, Anthony d'Offay Gallery, London
1997 *Changing Spaces. Artists' Projects from The Fabric Workshop and Museum, Philadelphia*, The Fabric Workshop and Museum, Philadelphia; Miami Art Museum; Arts Festival of Atlanta; 1998: The Detroit Institute of Arts; Vancouver Art Gallery
Sunshine & Noir. Art in L.A. 1960-1997, Louisiana Museum for Moderne Kunst, Humlebæk; Kunstmuseum Wolfsburg; 1998: Castello di Rivoli; UCLA at the Armand Hammer Museum of Art and Cultural Center, Los Angeles (cat.)
Kunst der Gegenwart, inaugural exhibition, Zentrum für Kunst und Medientechnologie Karlsruhe (cat.)
1998 *Geistes Gegenwart*, Diözesanmuseum, Freising, Germany (cat.)
'98 Kyongju Expo, Seoul (cat.)

On the occasion of the exhibition *The Magic of Trees*
Christo and Jeanne-Claude wrapped 162 deciduous
trees in and around the museum grounds.
Duration of the project:
November 21, 1998 – (presumably) January 24, 1998

Christo, *Drawing,* 1998, in two parts: 15 x 65" and
42 x 65"
Christo, *Drawing,* 1977, in two parts: 15¼ x 97½" and
42¾ x 97½" (pp. 172/173)

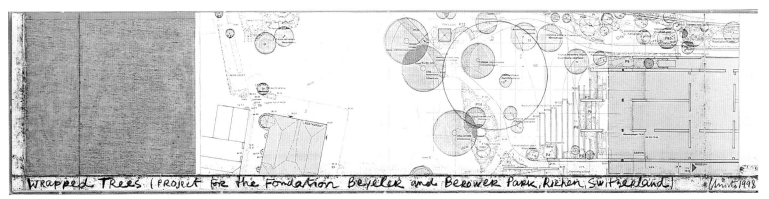

WRAPPED TREES (PROJECT FOR THE FONDATION BEYELER AND BEROWER PARK, RIEHEN, SWITZERLAND) *Christo* 1998

hight 14.56 m. diameter 14.5 m. CATALPA BIGNONIOIDES
height 11.91 m. From lowest branch to top.

height 2.55 m. From lowest branch to ground level

WRAPPED TREES (PROJECT FOR THE Fondation BEYELER and BEROWER P...

high 26.00 meter, diameter 13.00 meter

high 17.00 m.

Tilia Tomentosa, Tilia Cordata, Carpinus Betulus

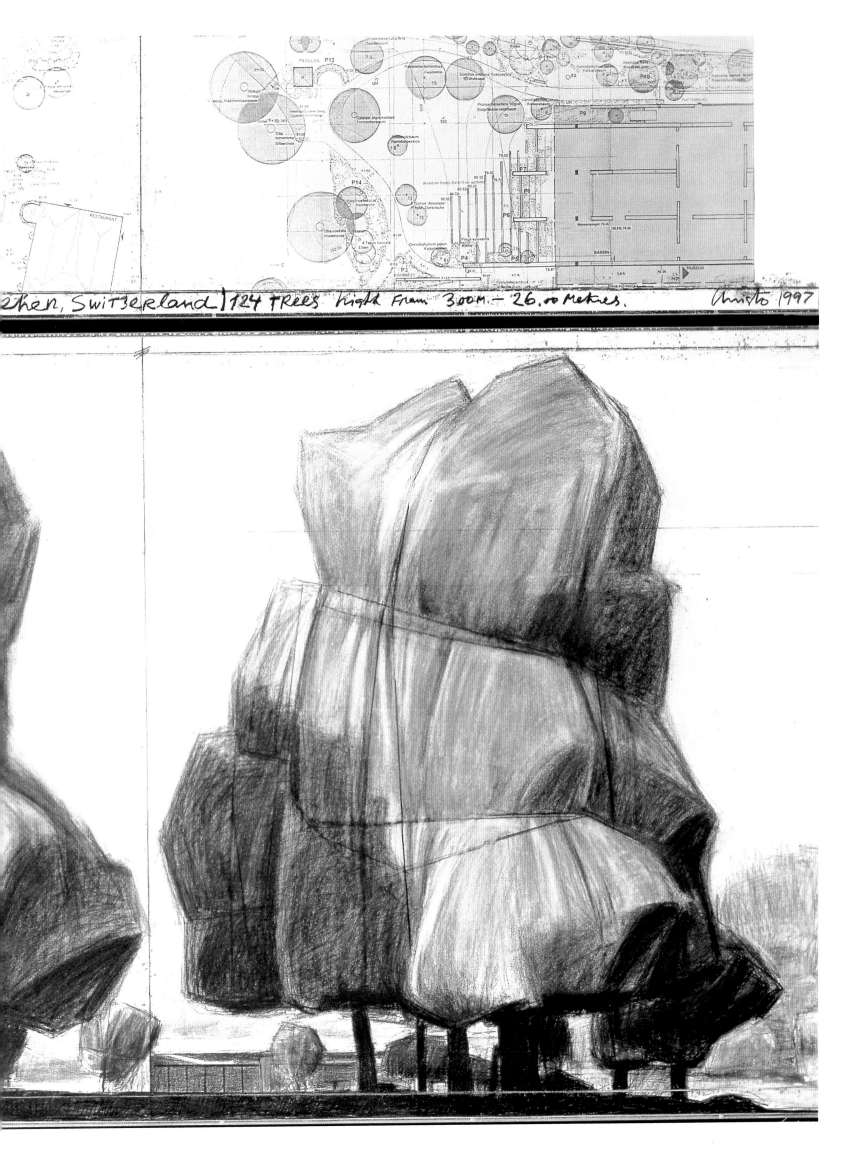

zhen, Switzerland] 124 TREES High From 3.00m - 26.00 Metres.   Christo 1997

Photo credit

Fondation Beyeler
Donations

On the occasion of the exhibition *The Magic of Trees* we would like to thank all those who donated generously to the planting of new trees in Berower Park at the time of the foundation's establishment.

Hildy and Ernst Beyeler

ARGE Maler- + Tapezierarbeiten, Frösch + Scherr AG/Steck AG, Basle
ARGE Gipserarbeiten Villa, Goepfert AG/ Grassi AG, Basle
ARGE Gipserarbeiten Museum, Grassi AG/ Stamm AG/Canonica + Lotti AG, Basle
ARGE Dachkonstruktion Jakem AG/G+H, Münchwilen
ARGE Naturstein Züblin AG/Tschudin AG, Basle
ARGE Fassade Nyfeler AG/Preiswerk und Esser AG/Gerber-Vogt AG, Basle
ARGE Parkett Stücker AG, Basle
ARGE Umgebung Fisch AG/Wenger AG/ Walo Bertschinger AG, Basle
Bammerlin + Schaufelberger AG, Riehen/Basle
Bator AG, Herzogenbuchsee
Baumann AG, Riehen/Basle
Bertschinger Walo AG, Basle
Bürgenmeier H., Riehen/Basle
Canonica + Lotti, Basle
Danzeisen Söhne AG, Basle
Dewag, Basle
Imbau AG, Basle
Lenzlinger Söhne AG, Uster
Müller Metallbau, Basle
RAG Brandabschottung, Gisikon
Schindler Lift AG, Basle
Securiton AG, Birsfelden
Sprecher + Kuster AG, Basle
Storama AG, Burgistein
Sulzer Infra AG, Basle
Tschudin AG, Schreinerei, Basle
Voellmy & Co. AG, Schreinerei, Basle
Wagner René, Riehen/Basle
Zihlmann AG, AV-Anlagen, Binningen
Züblin AG, Baumeister, Riehen/Basle

as well as all of the private donors who wish to remain anonymous

crossair
Official Carrier

S A R A S I N

Exhibition
Ernst Beyeler
Markus Brüderlin

Loans, realisation and coordination
Pascale Zoller, Susanne Kudielka, Oliver Wick
Verena Formanek, Delia Ciuha, Katharina Schell

Exhibition realisation
Verena Formanek, Bruno Guthauser, Ben Ludwig,
Urs Albrecht, Katharina Schell

Logistics
Beat Privat

Fondation Beyeler
Baselstr. 101
CH-4125 Riehen / Basle
Switzerland
Tel.: 0041 (0) 61 645 97 00
Fax: 0041 (0) 61 645 97 19
Internet: www.beyeler.com
e-Mail: fondation@beyeler.com

ISBN 3-905632-04-7 (English catalogue edition)
      3-905632-03-9 (German catalogue edition)
      3-905632-05-5 (French catalogue edition)

This book is published on the occasion of the exhibition *The Magic of Trees* in the Fondation Beyeler,
Riehen / Basle (November 21, 1998 – April 5, 1998)

Edited by
Fondation Beyeler

Editorial staff
Delia Ciuha, Susanne Kudielka, Pascale Zoller

German-English translations and proofreading
Judith Rosenthal

Design and production
Gerhard Brunner

Reproductions
Repromayer, Reutlingen

Overall production
Dr. Cantz'sche Druckerei, Ostfildern near Stuttgart

Published by
Verlag Gerd Hatje
Senefelderstraße 12
73760 Ostfildern-Ruit
Telephone (0)711 / 44 05 0
Telefax (0)711 / 44 05 220
Internet: www.hatje.de

ISBN 3-7757-0798-0 (English trade edition)
      3-7757-0803-0 (German trade edition)
      3-7757-0805-7 (French trade edition)

Printed in Germany

Jacket illustration
Pablo Picasso, *Landscape, La Rue-des-Bois,*
1908, plate p. 41

Front flap
Common oak (Quercus robur), ca. 500 years old, Italy
So-called »Witch oak«
The International Tree Archives, Verena Eggmann
1990

Back flap
Common beech (Fagus silvatica), ca. 300 years old,
France
The International Tree Archives, Verena Eggmann
1992